Getting Started with SharePoint Framework (SPFx)

Design and Build Engaging Intelligent Applications Using SharePoint Framework

by

Vipul Jain

FIRST EDITION 2020

Copyright © BPB Publications, India

ISBN: 978-81-94334-460

Distributors:

BPB PUBLICATIONS
20, Ansari Road, Darya Ganj
New Delhi-110002
Ph: 23254990/23254991

DECCAN AGENCIES
4-3-329, Bank Street,
Hyderabad-500195
Ph: 24756967/24756400

MICRO MEDIA
Shop No. 5, Mahendra Chambers,
150 DN Rd. Next to Capital Cinema,
V.T. (C.S.T.) Station, MUMBAI-400 001
Ph: 22078296/22078297

BPB BOOK CENTRE
376 Old Lajpat Rai Market,
Delhi-110006
Ph: 23861747

Published by Manish Jain for BPB Publications, 20 Ansari Road, Darya Ganj, New Delhi-110002 and Printed by him at Repro India Ltd, Mumbai

Dedicated to

My Beloved Family Members -
Your love and care are the foundation of my life!

About the Author

Vipul Jain is a result-oriented SharePoint Architect and Technical Project Manager with 10 years of experience in Microsoft Technologies, especially with SharePoint, Dot Net, and Microsoft Azure. He has been working with SharePoint for the last 10 years and has exposure to SharePoint versions starting from SharePoint 2007 (MOSS) till SharePoint 2019 and is leading many projects. He also has expertise in front-end web development and is also working and creating content on React JS.

He is a Microsoft Certified Professional with certifications in SharePoint, Office 365, and .Net. He is a regular contributor to SharePoint related articles and blogs on many websites and has experience in speaking in many technical events.

Acknowledgement

First and foremost, I would like to thank God. You have given me the power to believe in my passion and pursue my dreams. I would like to thank my mother, Mrs. Pushpa Jain, my father, Mr. Vijay Chand Jain, and family members for their endless support, blessings, care, and helping me in all possible ways.

I would like to give special thanks to my wife, Mrs. Muskan Jain, for her love, motivation, and guidance throughout the journey of writing this book. I could have never completed this book without her support.

I would like to thank my mentors for their useful inputs and suggestions, which helped me to write this book. I would like to thank everyone at BPB Publications for giving me the opportunity to write this book.

Lastly, I would like to thank all the readers of this book. It is because of you and your interest that I have had the opportunity to bring forth my thoughts about Getting Started with SharePoint Framework.

Preface

SharePoint Framework (SPFx) is a new option for developing SharePoint solutions. It has become the first choice for all SharePoint developers. This book explains how you can design, build, and deploy engaging applications using SharePoint Framework. You will learn about what is SharePoint Framework, how you can create modern solutions using open source and modern toolchain. The main goal of writing this book is to give knowledge on core concepts of SharePoint Framework. This book contains many examples with their screenshots and will be helpful to learn basic concepts of SharePoint Framework programming.

All examples in this book are based on SPFx version 1.10.0, which is the latest at the time of writing this book.

This book consists of 12 chapters in which you will learn the following:
Chapter 1, Getting started with SharePoint Framework, provides an overview of SharePoint Framework features and different programming models present for SharePoint development. This chapter describes the modern toolchain and flow of the client-side web part in SharePoint Framework applications. It also explains how you can set up your development environment to get started with SharePoint Framework.

Chapter 2, Develop the first client-side web part provides information on how you can start developing node-based projects, and then it gives you information about how you can create your first client-side web part using the Yeoman SharePoint generator and then how you can test your web part on local and SharePoint-hosted workbench.

Chapter 3, Understanding SharePoint Framework web part project structure, provides information about the solution structure of the SPFx client-side web part and major elements, files, and folders present inside the solution.

Chapter 4, Working with SharePoint Objects, is a key chapter that discusses, how you can add mock or sample data in the SPFx project and can test on a local workbench. Also, it tells you how you can access the SharePoint list and list items in SPFx web parts. It also gives you different ways to configure the SPFx web part icon.

Chapter 5, Working with SPFx Web Part Property Pane, is also a key chapter that guides you on how to create property panes in SPFx web parts and how you can change the data dynamically in SPFx web parts, based on property pane changes.

Chapter 6, Different hosting options for SPFx Web Part describes different Content Delivery Network options available for hosting or deploying your SPFx web parts.

Chapter 7, CRUD operations with different JavaScript frameworks introduce JavaScript framework options to implement CRUD operations in SPFx web parts. This chapter also presents a brief introduction to React JS.

Chapter 8, Logging, and Debugging in SPFx web parts describe Logging basics and different Logging API to be used in SPFx web parts. Also, this chapter will give you information about how you can debug your code in Visual Studio Code editor.

Chapter 9, SharePoint Framework Web part Examples describe SPFx web parts with a couple of examples. One of the examples tells you how you can implement a jQuery Accordion, and another example describes how you can build the Microsoft Teams tab using SharePoint Framework.

Chapter 10, Overview of SharePoint Framework Extensions explains different functionalities that can be implemented using SharePoint extensions. In this chapter, you will learn about different types of extensions, which are Application customizer, Field customizer, and Command Sets.

Chapter 11, Library Component Overview describes a new feature, i.e., Library Component Type of SharePoint Framework latest version. In this chapter, you will see how you can create a 3rd party SPFx library.

Chapter 12 gives you information about Frequently asked questions of the SharePoint Framework.

Downloading the code bundle and coloured images:

Please follow the link to download the
Code Bundle and the *Coloured Images* of the book:

https://rebrand.ly/o6kxg2r

Errata

We take immense pride in our work at BPB Publications and follow best practices to ensure the accuracy of our content to provide with an indulging reading experience to our subscribers. Our readers are our mirrors, and we use their inputs to reflect and improve upon human errors if any, occurred during the publishing processes involved. To let us maintain the quality and help us reach out to any readers who might be having difficulties due to any unforeseen errors, please write to us at :

errata@bpbonline.com

Your support, suggestions and feedbacks are highly appreciated by the BPB Publications' Family.

Table of Contents

CHAPTER 1
Getting Started with SharePoint Framework

As we know, the development patterns for Office 365 and SharePoint has gone through various turns, and the newest turn in that is the SharePoint Framework. So, the next question is, why do we need yet another development way for SharePoint? Why do we need a SharePoint Framework? You will find the answer to these questions in this and subsequent chapters, so let's get started!

Structure

In this chapter, we will cover the following topics:

- History of SharePoint Development
- Why SharePoint Framework is required
- Overview of SharePoint Framework
- Tools used in SharePoint Framework development
- Setting up your development environment

Objective

After studying this chapter, you should be able to:

- Understand the concept of SharePoint Framework

- Understand the modern toolchain
- Set up your development environment

History of SharePoint Development

SharePoint was launched as an on-premises product in 2001. Following is the image depicting different SharePoint versions:

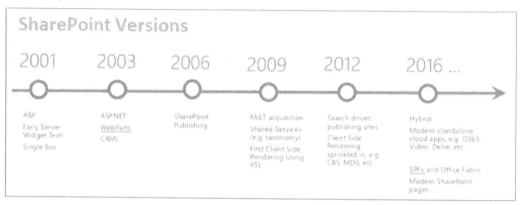

Figure 1.1

SharePoint 2019 is also launched by Microsoft.

The following are the primary development methods or techniques which we generally use while doing development in SharePoint:

- **Farm solutions:**

   The first development model in SharePoint started with farm solutions, writing full trust code, and deploying WSPs. This approach was compelling, and developers could do whatever they wanted to do on the SharePoint Farm using the server object model. Developers can create functionalities like timer jobs, event receivers, central administration extensions, and so on, using farm solutions. They can also create features that can have farm, web application, site collection, or website scope. However, it made upgrades very difficult, and it made maintaining and keeping the environment secure very difficult.

- **Sandboxed solutions:**

   As compared to farm solutions, the sandboxed solution has limited scope and limitations. It's like a box in which code cannot run outside the boundary of the box. Unlike farm solutions, sandboxed solutions scope is limited to a site collection only, and you cannot access objects above a site collection like a web application, farm, and so on. Whenever you create a sandboxed solution, the WSP file gets created in the **Solution Gallery** in **Site Settings**, and you can activate or deactivate the WSP based on the requirement.

Sandbox solution is no more developed in SharePoint on-premise and online development and being deprecated by Microsoft.

- **Add-ins (App Model):**

  It has been introduced in SharePoint 2013 and Office 365. It is based on iframe-based integration. This approach also has many disadvantages.

- **Script Injection:**

  Traditionally in classic SharePoint, you must have done Script Injection using Content Editor and Script Editor web-parts. With this approach, you can do almost everything on a SharePoint page; however, this is not the best-recommended approach.

- **No-script capability:**

  It is a tenant-widefull tenant setting that removes all content editor web-part and scripts from the page.

- **SharePoint Framework:**

  It is the new way of development in modern SharePoint. It is a custom and supported way from Microsoft, which allows embedding code inside SharePoint sites and pages. SharePoint Framework provides full support for client-side development and supports modern open-source toolchain like Yeoman, Gulp, and so on.

The following image gives a glimpse of different development methods or techniques discussed above:

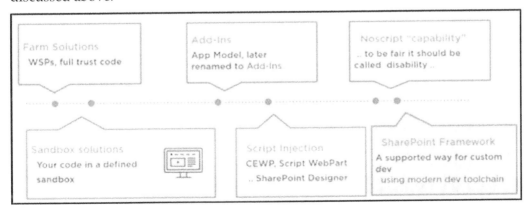

Figure 1.2

The landscape of SharePoint and Office 365 Development

So, with that, let's get started with the landscape of SharePoint and Office 365 development. Every SharePoint and Office 365 developer, or even business user, knows what web parts are. These are those canonical rectangular widgets or user-controls of pre-packaged functionality that the user can configure at runtime. Now the first release of the SharePoint Framework targeted this scenario. They called it client web parts. From a technology perspective, they are quite different, but from a user's standpoint, they are the same rectangular widgets that the users are used to dropping on the SharePoint pages.

Why SharePoint Framework?

The question arises here is – why SharePoint Framework? We have so many ways of developing for SharePoint. Why do you need yet another way of development for SharePoint? So, as we know that in the starting days of SharePoint development, there were feature XML files, however with time, these types of solutions didn't work well in the cloud (in terms of scaling) where multiple tenants run side-by-side. So, there are two main models that we generally use, that is, JavaScript injection and SharePoint Add-in model. Following are their pros and cons:

- **JavaScript injection:** As we know, the most popular web parts in SharePoint Online are the Content Editor and Script Editor web parts. We can paste JavaScript directly in the Script Editor web part and can pass JavaScript code to the Content Editor web part by writing code in a .txt, .html, or .JS file. Hence, code runs in the same browser context as that of page.

  The downside to this approach is that users can edit the page and can modify the code written in the Script Editor web part. Also, the Script Editor web part is not marked as "Safe For Scripting," which means the Script Editor web part will be blocked from executing on some of the sites like my-sites, team sites, and so on.

- **SharePoint Add-in model**: Add-in model or Apps are based on iFrame. As we know, iFrames are slower than Script Editor web part because it requires a new request to another page. So, the SharePoint page must go through authentication and authorization, load JavaScript's, and many more. Hence, an iFrame based page takes more time to load and ultimately affects performance (loading time) of a web page.

Overview of SharePoint Framework (SPFx)

SharePoint Framework is also termed as SPFx. SharePoint Framework uses modern open-source toolchain, Node-based development, TypeScript, and so on, that are used in SharePoint on-premise and Office 365 (SharePoint Online) development. SPFx is a page and web part model which works very well with SharePoint objects.

The following image shows some of the capabilities of SharePoint Framework like:

- Works in Office 365
- Allows you to write client-side web parts
- Uses modern tools and technologies

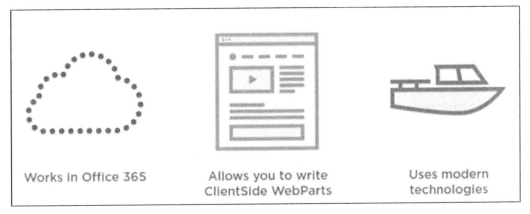

Works In Office 365

Allows you to write ClientSide WebParts

Uses modern technologies

Figure 1.3

SharePoint Framework works for SharePoint Online and on-premises (SharePoint 2016 Feature Pack 2 and SharePoint 2019).

Key features of SharePoint Framework are as follows:

- SPFX runs in the context of the current user and connection with the browser. No iFrames are used for customization purposes as JavaScript is embedded directly onto the page, which ultimately increases page performance.
- Faster rendering on the browser as all controls are rendered in the standard page DOM.
- Controls are responsive and accessible.
- Provides controls to access the lifecycle methods of a SharePoint Framework web part like Init, render, load, serialize, deserialize, and so on, and also allows developers to make configuration changes.
- SPFx is framework-agnostic, which means you can use any JavaScript framework of your choice, like React, Knockout, Angular, and so on.
- Open source development tools are used (npm, Typescript, Yeoman, Webpack, and Gulp).
- SPFx web parts can be added on both classic and modern SharePoint sites and pages.

- You can leverage your earlier knowledge of CSOM, as the data models are not changed and are completely transferable
- SPFx web parts are safe and secure, as the tenant administrator access level is required to make changes in the SPFx web part.

The following table shows the differences between Script Editor Web Parts, App Parts, and SPFx web part:

Script Editor Web Parts	App Parts	SPFx Web Parts
• The first choice of developers for customizing DOM on classic SharePoint sites • The script can be edited by any users easily • Cannot be added to "NoScript" sites	• Developed using Add-in model • Uses iframe • Cannot access DOM of SharePoint page • Development and deployment are bit complex	• Client-side web parts, leverages modern JavaScript frameworks • Can be used with classic SharePoint pages • SPFx web parts are by default responsive in nature

Table 1.1

Light-weight components/tools used in SPFx development

Following is a similar image showing the comparison between server-side and modern toolchain:

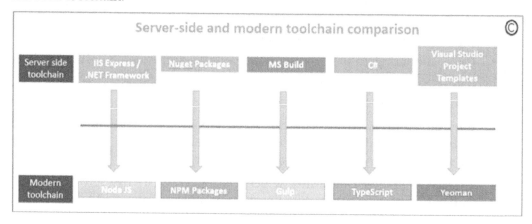

Figure 1.4

In the above image, we can see that as compared to previous server-side toolchains like IIS Express, NuGet packages, MS Build, C#, and so on, we will use their client-side open-source toolchain like node JS, npm packages, Gulp, Typescript and Yeoman for the same purposes.

To set up your development environment, node JS, Typescript, and an editor (like Visual Studio code) are the primary tools that need to be installed on your machine. Below is the explanation of the modern toolchain required for development in the SharePoint Framework.

Node.js

- Node.js is an open-source JavaScript runtime.
- It is lightweight and efficient.
- SPFx supports the latest **LTS (Long Term Support)** version

NPM

- 'NPM' stands for the node package manager.
- Required as a centralized package registry for SPFx.
- Installs modules and dependencies.
- Packages can be installed globally (using `-g`) or locally. Locally installed packages go in the `node_modules` subfolder.

Gulp

- Gulp is used to automate SPFx development and deployment tasks.
- Gulp can be used to automate repetitive build processes
- It is used as the task runner to handle build process tasks.
- Compiles SASS files to CSS
- Compiles TypeScript files to JavaScript
- Ability to compile, bundle, and copy files to deployment directories.

Yeoman

- Yeoman is used as a SharePoint web part generator.
- Yeoman builds out the project structure required; that is, Yeoman is the scaffolding tool for modern web apps.
- Yeoman relies on NPM and Gulp.
- yo is the Yeoman command line utility allowing the creation of projects.

Typescript

- Typescript is a strongly typed language

- Can catch and resolve syntax errors before run time. (Typescript adds compile-time syntax and types checking to JavaScript)
- It also supports writing classes and interfaces as required

Visual Studio Code

- Visual Studio code can be used for working with client-side web part projects
- Fast and lightweight IDE, which shows the file and folder structure of the project
- Visual Studio code is not the same as Visual Studio IDE
- It is available on Windows, Linux and Mac OS

The flow of client-side web part

The following diagram shows the flow of client-side web part from installation, development, and deployment and finally available on SharePoint pages:

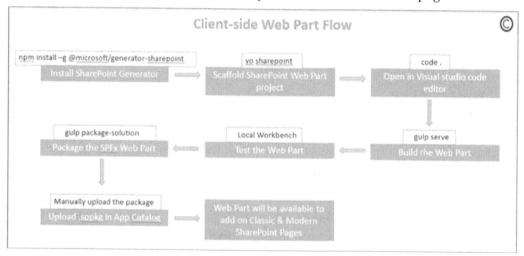

Figure 1.5

Set up Office 365 tenant

To build and deploy SPFx client-side web parts, you need an Office 365 tenant. You can get an Office 365 developer subscription by joining the Office 365 Developer Program (**https://developer.microsoft.com/en-us/office/dev-program**).

Use the following URL's to create free Office 365 tenant (without entering payment details) subscription for 30 days:

1. **Create Office 365 E5 trial tenant:** https://go.microsoft.com/fwlink/ p/?LinkID=698279

2. **Create Office 365 E3 trial tenant:** https://go.microsoft.com/fwlink/ p/?LinkID=403802

Create app catalog site

You will need an app catalog site to upload and deploy web parts. Follow the steps to create an app catalog site:

1. Go to the SharePoint admin center by entering the below URL in your browser. Replace yourtenantprefix with your Office 365 tenant prefix in the below URL: **https://yourtenantprefix-admin.sharepoint.com**

2. In the left sidebar, select **More features**, as shown in the following screenshot. Find the section **Apps** on the right-hand side and then click on **Open**:

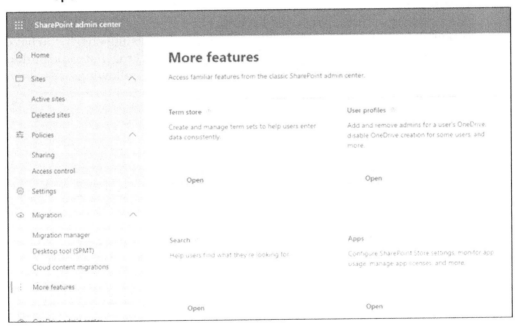

Figure 1.6

3. Once you are redirected to the **Apps** page, click on **App Catalog** and select **OK** create a new app catalog site:

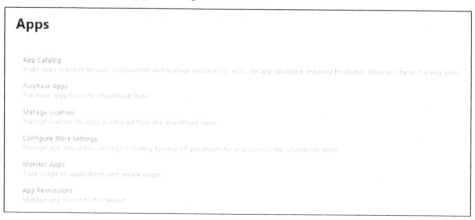

Figure 1.7

4. After clicking on **Apps**, you will be redirected to a screen asking for whether you want to create a new app catalog site or use the existing one. If you have not yet created an app catalog site in your tenant, select the first radio button to **Create a new app catalog site**, as shown in the following screenshot:

Figure 1.8

5. On the next page, enter the details, as shown in the following screenshot:

Figure 1.9

Take a brief of the following details:

- **Title:** Enter the title of your app catalog site; for example, App Catalog.
- **Web Site Address:** Enter your preferred suffix for the app catalog; for example, apps.
- **Administrator:** Enter your username, and then select the **Resolve** button to resolve the username.

6. Select **OK** to create the app catalog site. Once the site is created, you will be redirected to the app catalog site, as shown in the following screenshot:

Figure 1.10

Setting up your development environment

Once the app catalog site is created, create a site collection in your tenant by using the Team Site template.

SharePoint Workbench

Following are the key points related to SharePoint Workbench:

- SharePoint Workbench is a developer interface that allows developers to preview and test the client-side web parts without deploying them to SharePoint.
- It works with the current page context.

- Workbench is of two types: Local Workbench, which can be served locally in the browser, and SharePoint Workbench (or hosted workbench), which can be served from the SharePoint Online site.

- Local Workbench reloads whenever there is a change in code happens, which helps developers to view and update the web part dynamically. In other words, local workbench loads the SPFx version from your local toolchain.

  You can access SharePoint Workbench from any SharePoint site in your tenancy using the following URL: **https://your-sharepoint-site/_layouts/ workbench.aspx.**

The following is the set of commands required to get your developer environment ready for SPFx development.

Install Node JS

- Install the latest LTS version from **https://nodejs.org/en/download/.**
- If you already have NodeJS installed in your machine, check the version using the command:

  `node -v`

Below is the screenshot from my machine in which node JS version 10.16.3 is installed:

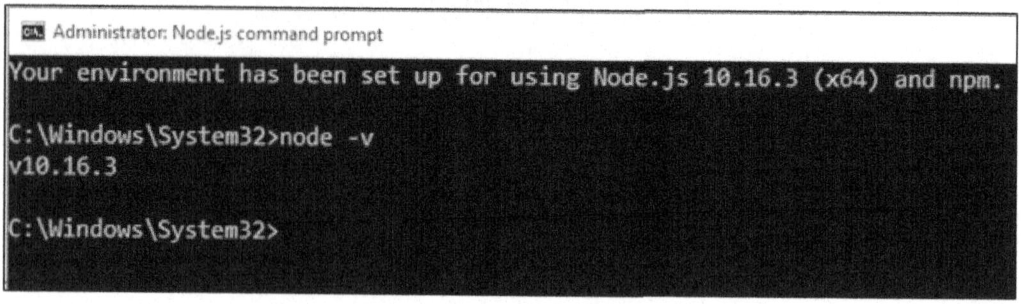

Figure 1.11

Install Yeoman and Gulp

- As we already know that Yeoman provides you project templates to start with your development, and Gulp works as the task manager in your SharePoint Framework solution. To install Yeoman and Gulp, use the following command to install them globally in your environment:

  `npm install -g yo gulp`

Below is the output of running the above command in my machine:

Figure 1.12

Install Code Editor

Any of the below code editors (or JavaScript development IDE's) can be freely chosen; however, the preferable one is Visual Studio Code:

1. Visual Studio Code **(https://code/visualstudio.com)**
2. Atom **(https://atom.io/)**
3. Webstorm **(https://www.jetbrains.com/webstorm)**
4. Sublime **(https://www.sublimetext.com/download)**

Install Yeoman SharePoint Generator

- The Yeoman SharePoint Framework solution generator helps you quickly create a SharePoint client-side solution project with the right toolchain and project structure.
- Use the following command to install the Yeoman SharePoint generator

```
npm i -g @microsoft/generator-sharepoint
```

Below is the screenshot from my machine after running the above command:

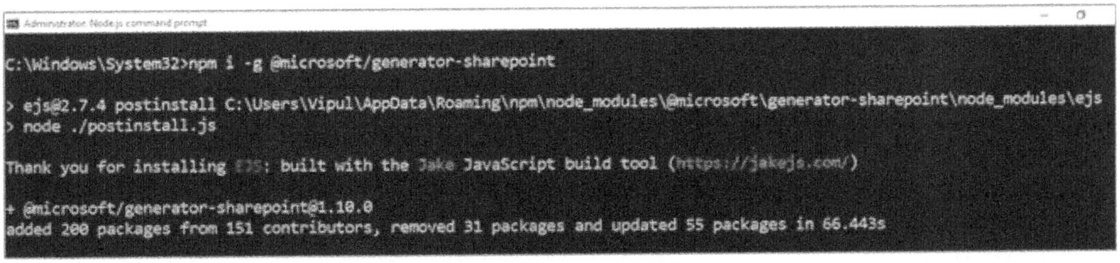

Figure 1.13

Check for updates

- Yo, Gulp, Yeoman SharePoint Generator gets installed as NPM packages. To make sure you are running the latest or updated version of NPM, use the following command:

```
npm install -g npm
```

Following is the output of above command which shows npm version 6.13.7:

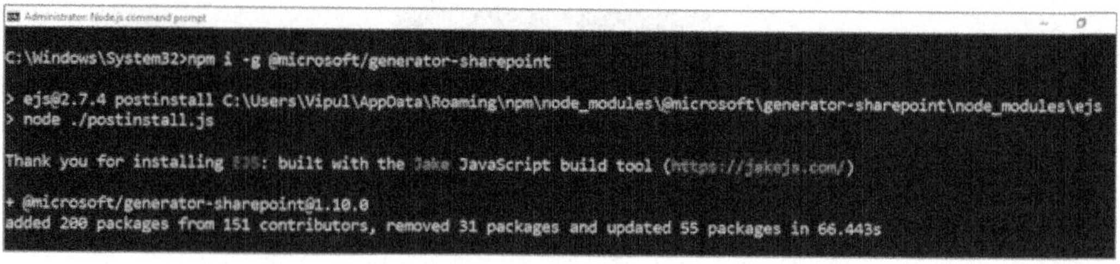

Figure 1.14

- To check outdated packages, use the following command. This command will tell which packages need to be updated:

npm outdated -global

Below is the output of above command which shows that webpack is not updated as the latest version is **4.41.5** and in my machine version **4.41.0** is installed:

Figure 1.15

- Use the below command to update the reported packages as per the previous command:

npm update -g <package-name>

Below is the output of above command which shows that webpack has been updated in my environment with the latest version 4.41.5:

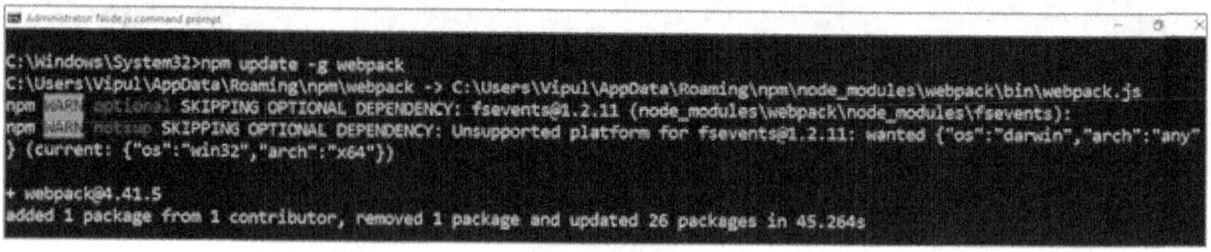

Figure 1.16

For installing packages, you can either use the keyword "install" or simply use "i."

Conclusion

In this chapter, we discussed the history of SharePoint and its evolution from one version to another. We also had a walkthrough on a high-level understanding of the SharePoint Framework and its key features. We also discussed the toolchain comparison and modern open-source toolchain, which will be used in the SharePoint Framework development. Finally, we saw how you could set up the development environment for getting started with SharePoint Framework development. In the next chapter, we will see how we can start with node-based development and can develop and test our first client-side web part.

Points to remember

- SharePoint Framework (SPFx) is a page and web part model which works very well with SharePoint objects.
- SPFX runs in the context of the current user.
- SPFx is framework-agnostic, which means you can use any JavaScript framework of your choice, like React, Knockout, Angular, and so on.

Multiple Choice Questions

1. What trust level do SharePoint Framework web parts run under:
   a. Add and remove pages permission
   b. Limited trust
   c. Same trust level as the user running them
   d. Manage permissions

2. Which of the below is untrue about SharePoint Framework:
   a. It does not work on classic sites
   b. SharePoint Framework can run server-side code
   c. It works on modern team sites
   d. You can develop for SharePoint Framework on a Mac machine

Answer

1. C
2. A

Questions

1. What is the difference between the script editor web part, app part, and SPFx web part?

2. Why is SharePoint Framework required?

3. What is the command to install Yeoman SharePoint Generator?

Key terms

*   Modern Toolchain: It refers to the open-source toolchain required for SharePoint Framework development.

CHAPTER 2

Develop First Client-Side Web Part

Client-side web parts developed using concepts of SharePoint Framework are the future and recommended way of modern SharePoint development. Client-side web parts support both SharePoint on-premise and online environments. Client-side web parts are developed using modern JavaScript, HTML, and libraries. They run inside the context of a SharePoint page.

In this chapter, you will learn how to develop your first client-side part using SharePoint Framework. Before reading this chapter, make sure to set up your development environment, as given in the previous chapter.

Structure

In this chapter, we will cover the following topics:

- Understanding NPM-based projects
- Develop the first client-side web part
- Installing the developer certificate
- Run web part on the local workbench

Objective

After studying this chapter, you should be able to:

- Understand the concept of SharePoint Framework
- Develop and test your first client-side web part using SharePoint Framework

Understanding NPM-based projects

Node-based or NPM based projects are the core of modern client-side development. In this section, we will learn how we can start with NPM based development and will understand the importance of different files.

NPM stands for the node package manager.

Follow the below steps to create an NPM based project:

1. Create a directory for the NPM based project:

   ```
   mkdir npmproject
   ```

2. Navigate to the directory created in *Step 1*:

   ```
   cd  npmproject
   ```

   The following screenshot shows the above two steps:

   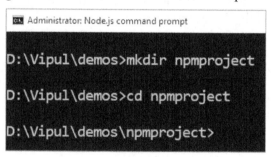

   Figure 2.1

3. Run the below command to create a file called `package.json`. If you do not hit `-yes`, then it will ask you many questions, so by default, I have given the default answer yes to all those questions:

   ```
   npm init -yes
   ```

The following screenshot shows the output of running the above command:

```
Administrator: Node.js command prompt

D:\Vipul\demos\npmproject>npm init --yes
Wrote to D:\Vipul\demos\npmproject\package.json:

{
  "name": "npmproject",
  "version": "1.0.0",
  "description": "",
  "main": "index.js",
  "scripts": {
    "test": "echo \"Error: no test specified\" && exit 1"
  },
  "keywords": [],
  "author": "",
  "license": "ISC"
}
```

Figure 2.2

Once the `package.json` file is created, we can see the file in folder structure also which we created earlier, as shown below:

Figure 2.3

Package.json is the central or main file for all node-based or npm-based projects. It can be considered as an introduction and setup file for your project. It contains dependencies, dev dependencies, scripts information. It also contains the name, version, description of the project.

4. Open the solution in code editor using below command, in my case; I am using Visual Studio Code:

    code

Below is the screenshot showing how to open your project in Visual Studio code. Note that after writing the command, press *Enter* to open the editor:

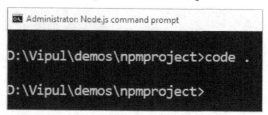

Figure 2.4

5. Now the `package.json` file is created, I will create a small program that will work with dates. We will use a library called `moment.js` and will add this library to the project. Run the below command to install `moment.js` in the project:

```
npm install moment -save
```

`--save` **is used so that package will appear in dependencies in** `package.json` **file. You can use** `-save-dev` **to add the package in dev dependencies in** `package.json` **file. For** `-save`, **you can also use** `-S`, **and for dev-dependencies, you can use** `-D`.

Below is the output of running the above command:

```
Administrator: Node.js command prompt

D:\Vipul\demos\npmproject>npm install moment --save
npm notice    created a lockfile as package-lock.json. You should commit this file.
npm WARN npmproject@1.0.0 No description
npm WARN npmproject@1.0.0 No repository field.

+ moment@2.24.0
added 1 package from 6 contributors and audited 1 package in 8.245s
found 0 vulnerabilities
```

Figure 2.5

This command will go online and will create the npm js registry and will modify the `package.json` file and will create a folder called `node_modules` in which `moment.js` file will be downloaded.

The folder name `node_modules` is very specific, and its recommended not to rename this folder.

Below is the screenshot of the modified `package.json` file having `moment.js` dependency and `node_modules` folder:

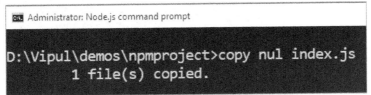

```
File  Edit  Selection  View  Go  Debug  Terminal  Help              package.json - npmproject - Visual Studio Code [Administrator]

  EXPLORER                      {} package.json ×
  ∨ OPEN EDITORS                {} package.json > ...
    ×  {} package.json            1  {
  ∨ NPMPROJECT                    2      "name": "npmproject",
    ∨ node_modules                3      "version": "1.0.0",
      ∨ moment                    4      "description": "",
        > locale                  5      "main": "index.js",
        > min                     6      "scripts": {
        > src                     7        "test": "echo \"Error: no test specified\" && exit 1"
        ⊙ CHANGELOG.md            8      },
        JS ender.js               9      "keywords": [],
        ▌ LICENSE                10      "author": "",
        TS moment.d.ts           11      "license": "ISC",
        JS moment.js             12      "dependencies": {
        JS package.js            13        "moment": "^2.24.0"
        {} package.json          14      }
        ⓘ README.md              15  }
    {} package-lock.json         16
    {} package.json
```

Figure 2.6

6. Create an empty file called `index.js` using the following command. In this file, we will write the code for `moment.js`:

   copy nul index.js

```
Administrator: Node.js command prompt

D:\Vipul\demos\npmproject>copy nul index.js
        1 file(s) copied.
```

Figure 2.7

7. Add the following code in the `index.js` file.

   ```
   var moment=require('moment');
   console.log(
       moment().format(
           'DD MMM YYYY, h:mm:ss a '
       )
   );
   ```

8. Since we are developing a node-based project, we can run the above code using the following command:

```
node index.js
```

The output of running the above command is shown below:

Figure 2.8

9. There is another way of running the above code. Go to the scripts section in the `package.json` file, and you can write as many scripts you want (by default, the test script is available). Here, we will write our script, let's say "`start`," as shown below:

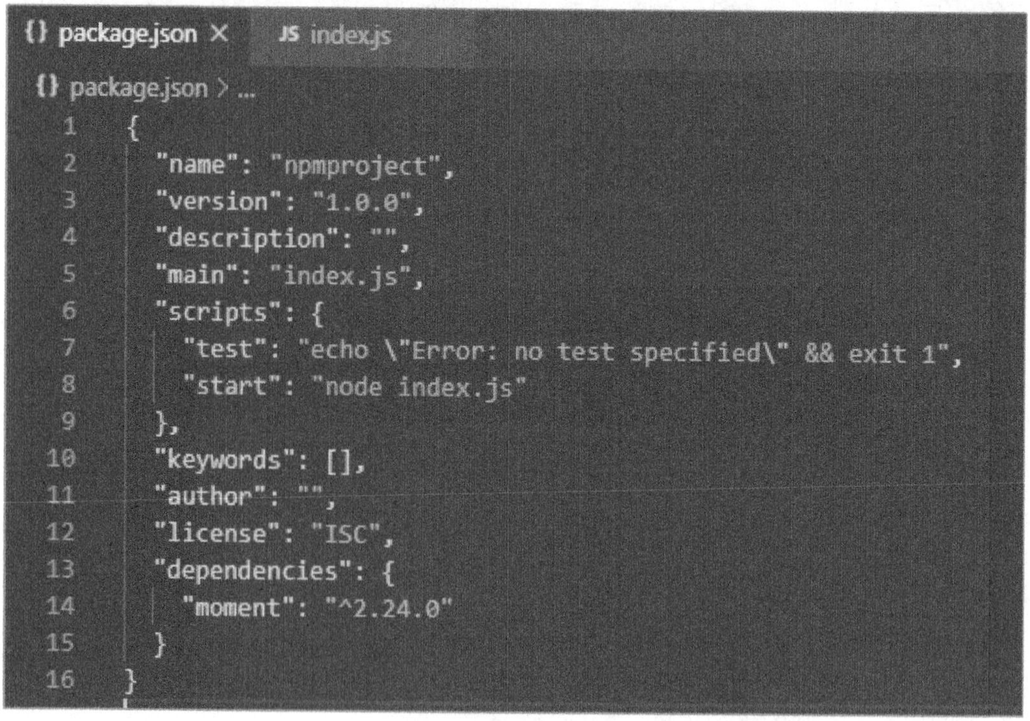

Figure 2.9

10. Rerun the code using the following command, and it should give you the same output as before:

```
npm start
```

The output of running the above command is shown below:

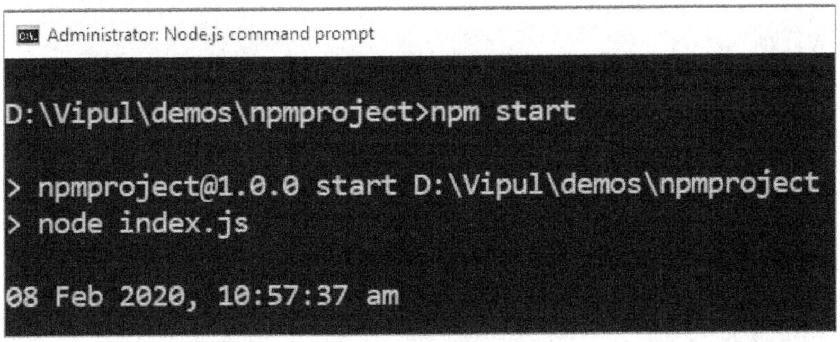

```
Administrator: Node.js command prompt

D:\Vipul\demos\npmproject>npm start

> npmproject@1.0.0 start D:\Vipul\demos\npmproject
> node index.js

08 Feb 2020, 10:57:37 am
```

Figure 2.10

Develop the first client-side web part

Follow the below steps to create your first web part project in SharePoint Framework:

1. Create a project directory for SPFx solution using the below command:

```
md firstspfx-webpart
```

You can either use mkdir or md for creating a new project directory.

2. Go to the project directory created in *Step 1* using the below command:

```
cd firstspfx-webpart
```

3. Run Yeoman SharePoint Generator using the below command to create the solution:

```
yo @microsoft/sharepoint
```

4. Once you run the above command, the Yeoman generator will ask some questions related to the solution to be created.

The following screenshot shows the output after running the Yeoman SharePoint Generator:

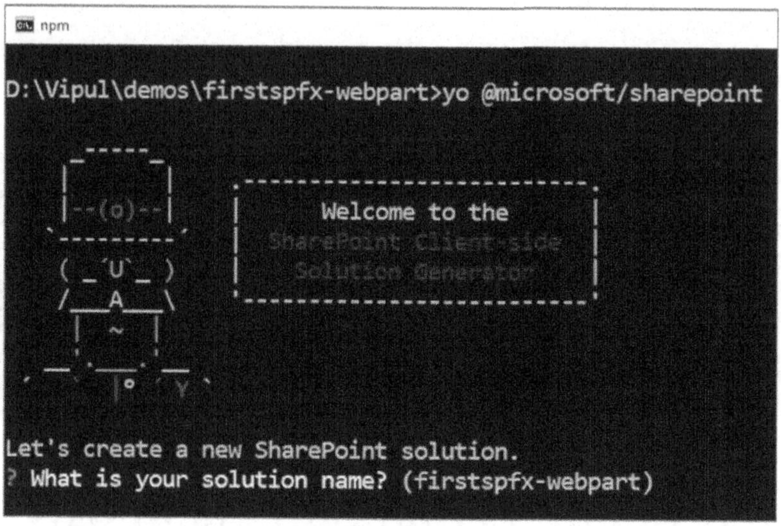

Figure 2.11

5. Below are the questions and selected choices for SharePoint Framework solution:

- **Solution Name:** You can either press *enter* to select the default solution name or write any other name of your solution.

  Choice selected: Press *Enter* key

- **The target for your component:** This option allows us to select the target environment where we will deploy the solution or client-side web part. The choices presented are SharePoint Online, SharePoint 2016 onwards and SharePoint 2019 onwards

  Choice selected: SharePoint Online only

- **Place of files:** This option allows us to use the same folder or create a subfolder for our solution.

  Choice selected: The same folder

- **Deployment:** This option allows us to decide whether the app should be deployed to all sites or install on each site explicitly.

  Choice selected: Y

- **Permissions:** This option allows us to choose permissions for the component to access Web APIs that are unique.

  Choice selected: N

- **Type of client-side component:** This option allows you to choose which client-side component you want to create, that is, WebPart, Extension, or Library.

  Choice selected: WebPart

  The following screenshot shows the options selected for different questions related to the solution:

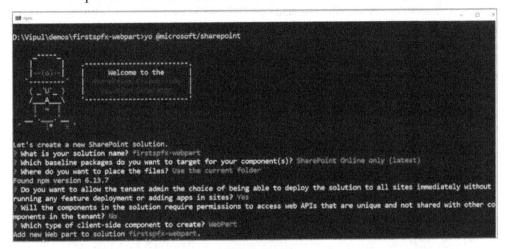

Figure 2.12

Once the above questions are answered, then questions will be presented related to the web part, which is covered in the next step.

6. Following are the questions and selected choices for SharePoint Framework web part in a solution:

- **Web part name:** Press *Enter* to select the default name, or you can write a different name for your web part.

  Choice selected: Press *Enter*

- **Web part description:** Press *Enter* to select the default description, or you can write a different description for your web part.

  Choice selected: Press *Enter*

- **JavaScript framework to use:** This option allows you to choose the JavaScript framework of your choice, that is, No JavaScript Framework, React, or Knockout.

  Choice selected: No JavaScript Framework

The following screenshot shows the options selected for different questions related to web part:

```
? What is your Web part name? HelloWorld
? What is your Web part description? HelloWorld description
? Which framework would you like to use? (Use arrow keys)
> No JavaScript framework
  React
  Knockout
```

Figure 2.13

7. After giving answers to all the questions, once you press enter, the Yeoman generator will start the scaffolding process to create the solution. It will install the required dependencies along with the HelloWorld web part. It might take a few minutes.

The following screenshot shows the different files which are getting created as part of the scaffolding process:

```
create package.json
create config\package-solution.json
create config\config.json
create config\serve.json
create tsconfig.json
create .vscode\extensions.json
create .vscode\launch.json
create .vscode\settings.json
create config\copy-assets.json
create config\deploy-azure-storage.json
create config\write-manifests.json
create src\index.ts
create gulpfile.js
create README.md
create tslint.json
create .editorconfig
create .gitignore
create src\webparts\helloWorld\HelloWorldWebPart.module.scss
create src\webparts\helloWorld\HelloWorldWebPart.ts
```

Figure 2.14

8. Once the scaffolding is done, Yeoman will show the below screen indicating a successful scaffold:

```
added 1743 packages from 1044 contributors and audited 745611 packages in 663.667s

21 packages are looking for funding
  run `npm fund` for details

found 1880 vulnerabilities (1831 low, 13 moderate, 36 high)
  run `npm audit fix` to fix them, or `npm audit` for details

     _=+#####|
  ###########|
  ###/   (##|(@)        -------------------------------------------
  ### #####|   \      |                Congratulations!              |
  ###/  /###|    (@) |    Solution firstspfx-webpart is created.    |
  ###### ##|   /     |       Run gulp serve to play with it!         |
  ###    /##|(@)       -------------------------------------------
  ###########|
    **=+####|

D:\Vipul\demos\firstspfx-webpart>
```

Figure 2.15

9. Open the solution in Visual Studio Code using the below command:

```
code
```

Installing the developer certificate

As we know, the client-side toolchain uses HTTPS endpoint by default, so we need to install the developer certificate. Install the developer certificate using the following command:

```
gulp trust-dev-cert
```

The following screenshot shows the output after running the above command:

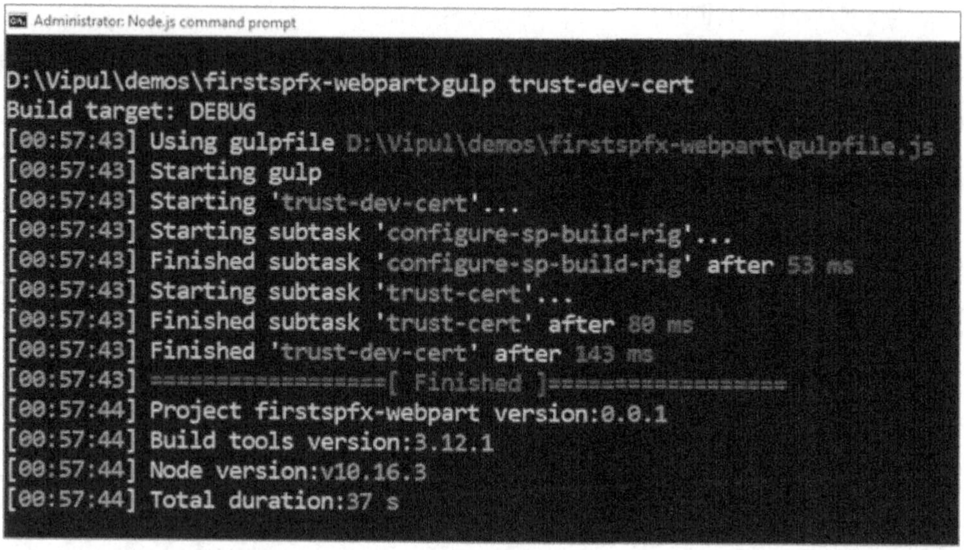

Figure 2.16

You need to install the developer certificate only once in your development environment.

Run the following command to build and preview your web part:

```
gulp serve
```

The following screenshot is the output of running the above command:

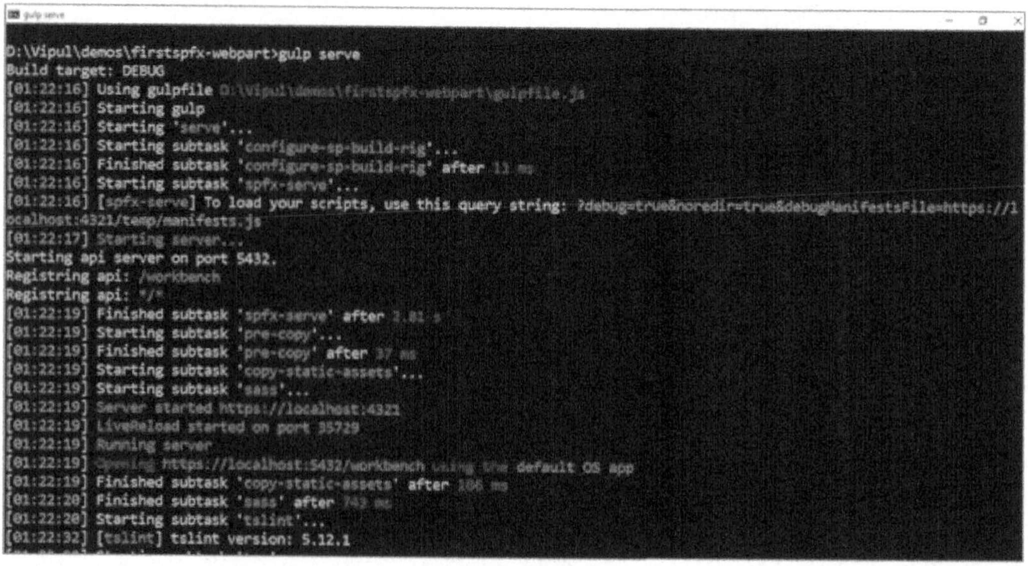

Figure 2.17

Gulp is used as a task runner which performs the below tasks:

- Minify and bundle JavaScript and CSS files
- Compiles **Sass (Syntactically Awesome Style Sheets)** to CSS
- Compiles TypeScript to JavaScript

Gulp tasks are defined and implemented in the `@microsoft\sp-build-core-tasks npm package`. Use the below command to list the different gulp tasks:

`gulp -T`

Below is the output of running the above command:

```
Administrator: Node.js command prompt

D:\Vipul\demos\firstspfx-webpart>gulp -T
[02:10:21] Tasks for D:\Vipul\demos\firstspfx-webpart\gulpfile.js
[02:10:21] ├── clean
[02:10:21] ├── build
[02:10:21] ├── default
[02:10:21] ├── bundle
[02:10:21] ├── dev-deploy
[02:10:21] ├── deploy-azure-storage
[02:10:21] ├── package-solution
[02:10:21] ├── test
[02:10:21] ├── serve
[02:10:21] ├── trust-dev-cert
[02:10:21] └── untrust-dev-cert
```

Figure 2.18

The various gulp tasks are as follows:

- `clean`: Deletes SharePoint Framework build folders and intermediate Sass files in the `src` folder
- `build`: Build the project
- `default`: Equivalent to a bundle
- `bundle`: Build, localize, and bundle the project
- `dev-deploy`: Deploy the current project to a development Azure CDN for sharing builds with colleagues
- `deploy-azure-storage`: Upload the assets to Azure storage container
- `package-solution`: Package the project into an SPPKG file
- `test`: build, localize, and bundle the project
- `serve`: Build and bundle the project and run the development server

- `trust-dev-cert`: Generates and trusts a development certificate if one isn't already present
- `untrust-dev-cert`: Untrusts and deletes the development certificate if it exists

Run web part on the local workbench

After the unbeaten run of gulp tasks, SharePoint local workbench will open. Click on (+) icon and select the web part to add on the page, as shown in the following screenshot:

Figure 2.19

The following screenshot shows the first client-side web part added on the page:

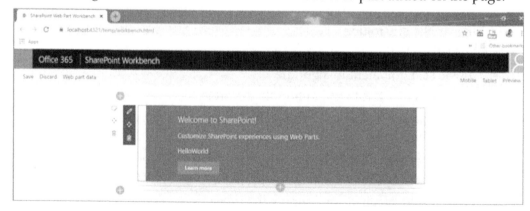

Figure 2.20

The above web part can be edited by clicking on the **Edit** icon. Modify description from properties pane, and it will be reflected on the client-side web part, as shown in the following screenshot:

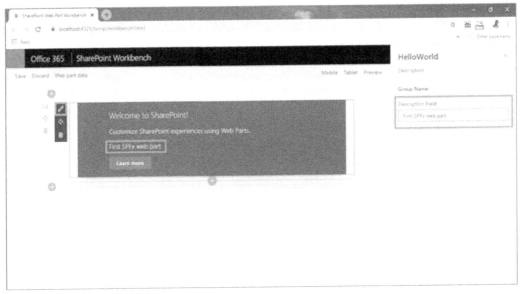

Figure 2.21

SharePoint local workbench gets served locally, usually on the below URL: **https://localhost:4321/temp/workbench.html.**

Conclusion

In this chapter, we discussed how to start development in NPM-based projects and also about the `package.json` file. We discussed client-side web parts and how you can develop your first client-side web part.

Points to remember

- Client-side web parts support both SharePoint on-premise and online environments and hence can be deployed to SharePoint Online also.
- Client-side web parts are developed using modern JavaScript, HTML, and libraries.
- Client-side web parts run inside the context of a SharePoint page.

Multiple Choice Questions

1. Which file describes the name and description of a node-based project:

    a. config.json

    b. package.json

    c. serve.json

    d. None of these

Answer

1. B

Questions

1. What is the command to run the Yeoman SharePoint Generator?

2. What is a developer certificate, and how can you install it locally?

Key terms

*   Client-side web part: It refers to the open-source toolchain required for SharePoint Framework development.

CHAPTER 3

Understanding SharePoint Framework Web Part Project Structure

We have seen in previous chapters that client-side web parts are lightweight, responsive, and can be developed using open-source toolchain like Node JS, NPM packages, Gulp, and Yeoman generators. Gulp is used as a task runner, NPM helps to install different modules or libraries, and the Yeoman generator helps in the scaffolding process.

In this chapter, you will learn about the different files and folders of a SharePoint Framework web part project.

Structure

In this chapter, we will cover the following topics:

- Understanding SharePoint Framework solution structure
- Main folders in the solution structure
- Essential files of the SharePoint Framework web part project
- Concept of SemVer

Objective

After studying this chapter, you should be able to:

- Understand the structure of a SharePoint Framework web part project

- Understand the use of different files and folders in a SharePoint Framework web part project

Understanding SharePoint Framework solution structure

Open the web part in the Visual Studio Code developed in the previous chapter using the following command:

```
code .
```

Below is the screenshot of the solution structure, which consists of various folders and files. The primary language used in SharePoint Framework development is Typescript, which is a superset of JavaScript. The main concepts of TypeScript are classes, modules, and interfaces:

Figure 3.1

Main folders in the solution structure

The following table briefs about the significance of all top-level folders visible in *Figure 3.1:*

Folder name	Description
.vscode	It includes Visual Studio Code integration files.
config	It includes all configuration related files.
dist	This folder is created automatically when you build the project, and it holds debug builds, also called distributable files (Typescript files which are compiled to JavaScript files.)
lib	This folder is created automatically when you build the project, and it contains the intermediate files which are used by SharePoint in the build process.
node_modules	This folder is created automatically when you build your project, and it includes all the NPM packages your solution relies upon and their dependencies.
src	It is the main folder of the project, as it includes the source code of the web part.
teams	This folder got introduced with the SharePoint Framework v1.8. This folder gets created during the scaffolding process and has default configurations of the web part, as it helps in teams-based development. By default, this folder contains two image files (small and large), which can be used as icons in Microsoft Teams based development.
temp	This folder is created automatically when you build your project, and it holds production builds.

Table 3.1

Essential files of the SharePoint Framework web part project

The following are the most critical files in the SPFx solution.

HelloWorldWebPart.ts (Web Part Class):

This file is located in the src | webparts | helloworld folder. This class represents the starting point, or we can say that this is the place where the execution begins. This class defines a property called IHelloWorldWebPartProps defined as an interface and is used to define custom property types of the web part. Each client-side web part extends from BaseClientSideWebPart, and this web part class also extends from the same parent class, that is, BaseClientSideWebPart.

The HelloWorldWebPart class contains the render() method, which renders the web part inside the DOM element.

render() method

We can access web part properties in `render()` method by using `this.properties.<value>` (For example, `${escape(this.properties.description)}`

> The HTML escape sequence is used on the property's value to ensure a valid string. If the property value does not return a valid string, you need to convert the value in a valid string explicitly.

Below is the screenshot of the `render()` method:

```
public render(): void {
  this.domElement.innerHTML = `
    <div class="${ styles.helloWorld}">
      <div class="${ styles.container}">
        <div class="${ styles.row}">
          <div class="${ styles.column}">
            <span class="${ styles.title}">Welcome to SharePoint!</span>
            <p class="${ styles.subTitle}">Customize SharePoint experiences using Web Parts.</p>
            <p class="${ styles.description}">${escape(this.properties.description)}</p>
            <a href="https://aka.ms/spfx" class="${ styles.button}">
              <span class="${ styles.label}">Learn more</span>
            </a>
          </div>
        </div>
      </div>
    </div>`;
}
```

Figure 3.2

Following is the method where we define web part property pane properties or configurations:

getPropertyPaneConfiguration

The properties are defined in `HelloWorldWebPart.ts` file in the `getProperty PaneConfiguration` section. By default, it contains one property; however, you can add multiple properties in this section.

The following screenshot shows the default property:

```
protected getPropertyPaneConfiguration(): IPropertyPaneConfiguration {
    return {
        pages: [
            {
                header: {
                    description: strings.PropertyPaneDescription
                },
                groups: [
                    {
                        groupName: strings.BasicGroupName,
                        groupFields: [
                            PropertyPaneTextField('description', {
                                label: strings.DescriptionFieldLabel
                            })
                        ]
                    }
                ]
            }
        ]
    };
}
```

Figure 3.3

HelloWorldWebPart.manifest.json (Web Part Manifest file)

This files stores web part metadata such as ID, component type, display name, description, icon, default properties, and so on. Every web part should contain one manifest file.

The following is the default JSON code of this file:

```
src > webparts > helloWorld > {} HelloWorldWebPart.manifest.json
1   {
2       "$schema": "https://developer.microsoft.com/json-schemas/spfx/client-side-web-part-manifest.schema.json",
3       "id": "67657205-7845-4b07-9429-42c733cb3b71",
4       "alias": "HelloWorldWebPart",
5       "componentType": "WebPart",
6
7       // The "*" signifies that the version should be taken from the package.json
8       "version": "*",
9       "manifestVersion": 2,
10
11      // If true, the component can only be installed on sites where Custom Script is allowed.
12      // Components that allow authors to embed arbitrary script code should set this to true.
13      // https://support.office.com/en-us/article/Turn-scripting-capabilities-on-or-off-1f2c515f-5d7e-448a-9fd7-835da935584
14      "requiresCustomScript": false,
15      "supportedHosts": ["SharePointWebPart"],
16
17      "preconfiguredEntries": [{
18          "groupId": "5c03119e-3074-46fd-976b-c60198311f70", // Other
19          "group": { "default": "Other" },
20          "title": { "default": "HelloWorld" },
21          "description": { "default": "HelloWorld description" },
22          "officeFabricIconFontName": "Page",
23          "properties": {
24              "description": "HelloWorld"
25          }
26      }]
27  }
28
```

Figure 3.4

config.json

This file contains information about your bundle(s) and any external dependencies (like jQuery) and localized resources. It also contains information about different components used in the solution and the entry point of the SPFx solution.

Following is the default JSON code of this file:

```
config > {} config.json > ...
1    {
2        "$schema": "https://developer.microsoft.com/json-schemas/spfx-build/config.2.0.schema.json",
3        "version": "2.0",
4        "bundles": {
5            "hello-world-web-part": {
6                "components": [
7                    {
8                        "entrypoint": "./lib/webparts/helloworld/HelloWorldWebPart.js",
9                        "manifest": "./src/webparts/helloworld/HelloWorldWebPart.manifest.json"
10                   }
11               ]
12           }
13       },
14       "externals": {},
15       "localizedResources": {
16           "HelloWorldWebPartStrings": "lib/webparts/helloworld/loc/{locale}.js"
17       }
18   }
```

Figure 3.5

deploy-azure-storage.json

This file is used while deploying the client-side web part to **Azure CDN (Content Delivery Network).** This file contains Azure storage account details.

The following screenshot is the default JSON code of this file:

```
config > {} deploy-azure-storage.json > ...
1    {
2        "$schema": "https://developer.microsoft.com/json-schemas/spfx-build/deploy-azure-storage.schema.json",
3        "workingDir": "./temp/deploy/",
4        "account": "<!-- STORAGE ACCOUNT NAME -->",
5        "container": "firstspfx-webpart",
6        "accessKey": "<!-- ACCESS KEY -->"
7    }
```

Figure 3.6

package-solution.json

This file contains solution path configurations.

The following screenshot is the default JSON code of this file:

```
config > {} package-solution.json > ...
  1   {
  2     "$schema": "https://developer.microsoft.com/json-schemas/spfx-build/package-solution.schema.json",
  3     "solution": {
  4       "name": "firstspfx-webpart-client-side-solution",
  5       "id": "ade292cd-16db-4a10-9643-d2c53c8ab474",
  6       "version": "1.0.0.0",
  7       "includeClientSideAssets": true,
  8       "skipFeatureDeployment": true,
  9       "isDomainIsolated": false
 10     },
 11     "paths": {
 12       "zippedPackage": "solution/firstspfx-webpart.sppkg"
 13     }
 14   }
```

Figure 3.7

package.json

This file contains information about your project (name, version, and so on), and it lists the dependencies and dev-dependencies that your project is dependent on.

Below is the default JSON code of this file:

```
{} package.json > ...
  1   {
  2     "name": "firstspfx-webpart",
  3     "version": "0.0.1",
  4     "private": true,
  5     "main": "lib/index.js",
  6     "engines": {
  7       "node": ">=0.10.0"
  8     },
  9     "scripts": {
 10       "build": "gulp bundle",
 11       "clean": "gulp clean",
 12       "test": "gulp test"
 13     },
 14     "dependencies": {
 15       "@microsoft/sp-core-library": "1.10.0",
 16       "@microsoft/sp-property-pane": "1.10.0",
 17       "@microsoft/sp-webpart-base": "1.10.0",
 18       "@microsoft/sp-lodash-subset": "1.10.0",
 19       "@microsoft/sp-office-ui-fabric-core": "1.10.0",
 20       "@types/webpack-env": "1.13.1",
 21       "@types/es6-promise": "0.0.33"
 22     },
 23     "devDependencies": {
 24       "@microsoft/sp-build-web": "1.10.0",
 25       "@microsoft/sp-tslint-rules": "1.10.0",
 26       "@microsoft/sp-module-interfaces": "1.10.0",
 27       "@microsoft/sp-webpart-workbench": "1.10.0",
 28       "@microsoft/rush-stack-compiler-3.3": "0.3.5",
 29       "gulp": "~3.9.1",
 30       "@types/chai": "3.4.34",
 31       "@types/mocha": "2.2.38",
 32       "ajv": "~5.2.2"
 33     }
```

Figure 3.8

package-lock.json

This file gets automatically generated while installing node packages. This file is helpful when someone clones your solution using `npm install` command, then NPM will look into `package-lock.json` and will install exact versions of the package you have installed and hence will ignore the ^ and ~ versions from `package.json`.

gulpfile.js

This file defines various gulp tasks to be run.

tsconfig.json

This file defines settings for TypeScript compilation.

Concept of SemVer

SemVer stands for semantic versioning. The idea behind semantic versioning is that a version is associated with each NPM package and is represented as "a.b.c." This representation has the following meaning:

- "a" means that you are shipping a significant version that could break the existing code. In that case, this number gets updated.
- "b" means that you are making changes in the API in terms of adding new methods, new features that will not break the existing code. In that case, this digit gets updated.
- "c" means if you are just issuing a path (or bug fixes), which means there are no changes in the API. In that case, this digit gets updated.

The following image shows the concept of SemVer diagrammatically:

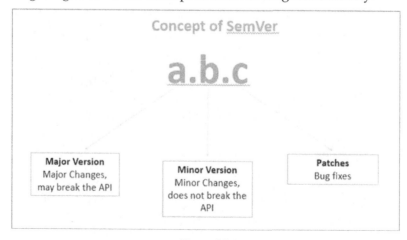

Figure 3.9

We can see the dependencies of different NPM packages in the `package.json` file and are added in the following ways:

- **Caret dependency:** Any version up to (but not including) is accepted, which means for Caret dependency, only major version should match, and any minor or patch version greater than or equal to the minimum is valid.

  Example: ^3.2.1 means greater than or equal to 3.2.1

- **Tilde dependency:** It is similar to Caret dependency, but the range is small, which means for Tilde dependency, major and minor versions must match with those specified; however, any patch version greater than or equal to the one specified is valid.

  Example: ~3.2.1 means greater than or equal to 3.2.1

- **Exact dependency:** Constrained to a specific version.

  Example: 3.2.1 means 3.2.1 only

Conclusion

In this chapter, we discussed different files and folders which get created with the SharePoint Framework solution and their significance as it is essential to understand the functionality of each file for a better level of development.

Points to remember

- The `src` folder contains all source code files.
- The `package-solution.json` file contains solution path configurations.
- The `deploy-azure-storage.json` file contains Azure storage account details.

Multiple Choice Question

1. Which folder contains configuration related files:
   a. config
   b. lib
   c. dist
   d. temp

Answer

1. A

Questions

a. How can you access web part properties in the SPFx web part solution and in which method?

b. What is the use of the team's folder?

c. What is Semantic Versioning?

Key terms

- node_modules: This folder is created automatically when you build your project; it includes all the NPM packages your solution relies upon and their dependencies.

CHAPTER 4

Working with SharePoint Objects

In the previous chapter, we discussed the SharePoint Framework web part solution structure and about the different file sand folder which gets created after the scaffolding process.

In this chapter, you will learn how the SPFx web part can be leveraged by connecting to SharePoint. You will also learn how to change the SPFx web part icon and how you can play around with mock or sample data and can test the functionality in SharePoint local workbench.

Structure

In this chapter, we will cover the following topics:

- How to access page context
- Using mock data with local and hosted workbench
- Deploy web part on a SharePoint Page
- Configure SPFx Web Part Icon

Objective

After studying this chapter, you should be able to:

- Leverage mock or sample data in a SharePoint Framework web part project

- Test the web part in local and SharePoint workbench
- Change SPFx web part icon

Access Page Context

In this section, we will discuss how to access page context in a SharePoint Framework web part.

Open the solution created in the previous chapter in Visual Studio Code and go to render method in `HelloWorldWebPart.ts` file. The following screenshot shows the default render method (which comes with SPFx web part):

```
public render(): void {
  this.domElement.innerHTML = `
    <div class="${ styles.helloWorld}">
      <div class="${ styles.container}">
        <div class="${ styles.row}">
          <div class="${ styles.column}">
            <span class="${ styles.title}">Welcome to SharePoint!</span>
            <p class="${ styles.subTitle}">Customize SharePoint experiences using Web Parts.</p>
            <p class="${ styles.description}">${escape(this.properties.description)}</p>
            <a href="https://aka.ms/spfx" class="${ styles.button}">
              <span class="${ styles.label}">Learn more</span>
            </a>
          </div>
        </div>
      </div>
    </div>`;
}
```

Figure 4.1

Inside the `render` method, add the below HTML code, as shown in the following screenshot:

```
<p class="${ styles.description }">Loading from ${escape(this.context.
pageContext.web.title)} </p>
```

```
public render(): void {
  this.domElement.innerHTML = `
    <div class="${ styles.helloWorld}">
      <div class="${ styles.container}">
        <div class="${ styles.row}">
          <div class="${ styles.column}">
            <span class="${ styles.title}">Welcome to SharePoint!</span>
            <p class="${ styles.subTitle}">Customize SharePoint experiences using Web Parts.</p>
            <p class="${ styles.description}">${escape(this.properties.description)}</p>
            <p class="${ styles.description }">Loading from ${escape(this.context.pageContext.web.title)}</p>
            <a href="https://aka.ms/spfx" class="${ styles.button}">
              <span class="${ styles.label}">Learn more</span>
            </a>
          </div>
        </div>
      </div>
    </div>`;
}
```

Figure 4.2

In the above screenshot, we have added an extra `<p>` tag to display the title of the page using `this.context.pageContext.web.title`. This line of code will display the title as `Local Workbench` when we run it in SharePoint local workbench. However, when the above code is run in SharePoint hosted workbench, the output will be web site title.

SharePoint workbench page context provides below fundamental properties:

- **Web title**
- **Web absolute URL**
- **Web server-relative URL**
- **User sign-in name**

Save the file and make sure that you have the `gulp serve` command running. If it is not running, then go to the `helloworld-webpart` project directory and run as shown in the following screenshot:

Figure 4.3

The `gulp serve` command performs the following operations:

- It builds and bundles the code automatically
- It refreshes your local workbench page as and when the web part code is updated

Output:

Once `gulp serve` runs all its tasks, it will open local workbench (in your default browser) and will show the output as shown in the following screenshot:

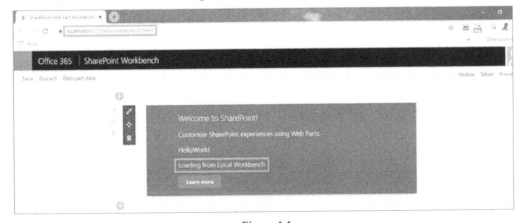

Figure 4.4

SharePoint local workbench gets loaded on the URL `https://localhost:4321/temp/workbench.html`.

To see the output in SharePoint, navigate to your SharePoint site and open SharePoint workbench using the following URL **https://your-sharepoint-site-url/_layouts/workbench.aspx**.

In my case, I created a modern Team Site (which is also a site collection) and the output is shown in the following screenshot:

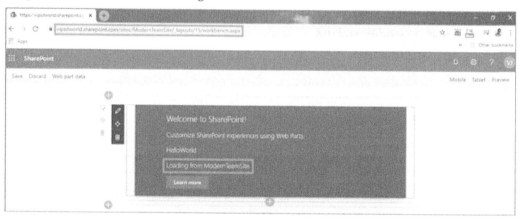

Figure 4.5

Using mock data with local and hosted workbench

In this section, you will see how you can add mock or sample data, define list model and can test the web part in local and SharePoint hosted workbench.

Follow the below steps to develop and test the web part:

1. Go to `HelloWorlWebPart.ts` file (`src | webparts | helloWorld | HelloWorldWebPart.ts`) and define the following interfaces just above the `HelloWorldWebPart` class:

```
export interface ISPLists {

  value: ISPList[];

}
export interface ISPList {

  Title: string;

  Id: string;

}
```

The `ISPLists` interface is used for mock data, and the `ISPList` interface holds the SharePoint list information.

2. In this step, we will add the mock or sample data so that the web part can be tested in local workbench. Create a new file inside the `src` | `webparts` | `helloWorld` folder named `SampleData.ts` and copy the following code in `SampleData.ts` file:

```
import { ISPList } from './HelloWorldWebPart';

export default class SampleData  {


    private static _items: ISPList[] = [{ Title: 'Mock Data 1',
Id: '1' },
                                        { Title: 'Mock Data 2',
Id: '2' },
                                        { Title: 'Mock Data 3',
Id: '3' }];


    public static get(): Promise<ISPList[]> {
    return new Promise<ISPList[]>((resolve) => {
            resolve(SampleData._items);
        });
    }

}
```

3. Save the file. Now to consume the `SampleData.ts` in the main web part file, we need to import the sample file, that is, `SampleData.ts`. Import the `SampleData.ts` file using the below command. Write the following command just under `import * as strings from 'HelloWorldWebPartStrings'`:

```
import SampleData from './SampleData';
```

Following is the screenshot showing the above steps:

```
TS HelloWorldWebPart.ts ×    TS SampleData.ts

src > webparts > helloWorld > TS HelloWorldWebPart.ts > ...
  1    import { Version } from '@microsoft/sp-core-library';
  2    import {
  3      IPropertyPaneConfiguration,
  4      PropertyPaneTextField
  5    } from '@microsoft/sp-property-pane';
  6    import { BaseClientSideWebPart } from '@microsoft/sp-webpart-base';
  7    import { escape } from '@microsoft/sp-lodash-subset';
  8
  9    import styles from './HelloWorldWebPart.module.scss';
 10    import SampleData from './SampleData';
 11    import * as strings from 'HelloWorldWebPartStrings';
 12
 13    export interface IHelloWorldWebPartProps {
 14      description: string;
 15    }
 16
 17    export interface ISPLists {
 18      value: ISPList[];
 19    }
 20    |
 21    export interface ISPList {
 22      Title: string;
 23      Id: string;
 24    }
```

Figure 4.6

4. Modify `HelloWorldWebPart.ts` file by adding a `private` method using the following code. These methods mocks or calls the sample data:

```
private _getMockListData(): Promise<ISPLists> {

  return SampleData.get()

    .then((data: ISPList[]) => {

      var listData: ISPLists = { value: data };

      return listData;

    }) as Promise<ISPLists>;

}
```

5. In this step, we will retrieve all lists in a SharePoint site using SharePoint REST APIs and will use the below endpoint URL **https://yourtenantprefix. sharepoint.com/_api/web/lists.**

In SharePoint Framework, all REST API and HttpContext related operations are available in the @microsoft/sp-http package or module. This package contains a helper class called **spHttpClient**, which helps in executing REST API calls and has inbuilt GET and POST methods, which helps in making calls to SharePoint. These methods automatically add headers to GET and POST requests.

6. Use the following code to import SPHttpClient and SPHttpClientResponse from @microsoft/sp-http package. You can write the below code just under the import command for SampleData.ts file, as shown in the following screenshot:

```
import {
    SPHttpClient,
    SPHttpClientResponse
} from '@microsoft/sp-http';
```

Figure 4.7

The other important classes in package @microsoft/sp-http **are** : SPHttp ClientConfiguration, ODataVersion **and** ISPHttpClientConfiguration.

7. Like we added the method in *Step 4* to get the mock data, in this step we will add a private method to get the data from SharePoint site. Add the following private method in HelloWorldWebPart.ts file:

```
private _getListData(): Promise<ISPLists> {
    return this.context.spHttpClient.get(this.context.pageContext.
web.absoluteUrl + `/_api/web/lists?$filter=Hidden eq false`,
SPHttpClient.configurations.v1)
        .then((response: SPHttpClientResponse) => {
            return response.json();
        });
}
```

In this method, we have use `SPHttpClient` class and used it's GET method to retrieve the SharePoint lists (excluding hidden lists). Also, `ISPLists` interface is used in this method which we added in *Step 1* and we have used the configuration as `SPHttpClient.configurations.v1`. This configuration sets the below headers to your REST request and you don't have to set any headers manually:

```
consoleLogging = true;

jsonRequest = true;

jsonResponse = true;

defaultSameOriginCredentials = true;

defaultODataVersion = ODataVersion.v4;

requestDigest = true
```

8. You can add styling to your web part by making changes in the SCSS file, which comes with the SharePoint Framework web part solution. Open `HelloWorldWebPart.module.scss` file where you will define your styles. Add the following styles after the `.button` style, but still inside the main `.helloWorld` style section and save the file:

```
.list {
  color: #333333;
  font-family: 'Segoe UI Regular WestEuropean', 'Segoe UI',
Tahoma, Arial, sans-serif;
  font-size: 14px;
  font-weight: normal;
  box-sizing: border-box;
  margin: 10;
  padding: 10;
  line-height: 50px;
  list-style-type: none;
  box-shadow: 0 4px 4px 0 rgba(0, 0, 0, 0.2), 0 25px 50px 0
rgba(0, 0, 0, 0.1);
}

.listItem {
  color: #333333;
  vertical-align: center;
```

```
    font-family: 'Segoe UI Regular WestEuropean', 'Segoe UI',
Tahoma, Arial, sans-serif;

    font-size: 14px;

    font-weight: normal;

    box-sizing: border-box;

    margin: 0;

    padding: 0;

    box-shadow: none;

    *zoom: 1;

    padding: 9px 28px 3px;

    position: relative;

}
```

9. In the above steps, we have defined interfaces, mock data, private methods, and styling to test the web part both in local and SharePoint workbench; however, the question arises that how SharePoint Framework understands the environment where the code needs to be run. So, SharePoint Framework achieves this capability using the `EnvironmentType` module.

Import the Environment and the `EnvironmentType` modules from the `@ microsoft/sp-core-library` package using the following code:

```
import {

  Environment,

  EnvironmentType

} from '@microsoft/sp-core-library';
```

Add the above code in the import section in `HelloWorldWebPart.ts` file, as shown in the following screenshot:

```
10    import SampleData from './SampleData';
11
12    import {
13      SPHttpClient,
14      SPHttpClientResponse
15    } from '@microsoft/sp-http';
16
17    import {
18      Environment,
19      EnvironmentType
20    } from '@microsoft/sp-core-library';
21
```

Figure 4.8

10. In this step, we will add a `private` method that will be used to render list information and will use the new CSS styles defined in *Step 8*. Use the below code to add a `private` method in main web part file:

```
private _renderList(items: ISPList[]): void {
  let html: string = '';
  items.forEach((item: ISPList) => {
    html += `
<ul class="${styles.list}">
  <li class="${styles.listItem}">
    <span class="ms-font-l">${item.Title}</span>
  </li>
</ul>`;
  });


  const listContainer: Element = this.domElement.
querySelector('#spListContainer');
  listContainer.innerHTML = html;
}
```

11. Now we have two private methods as defined in *Step 4* and *Step 7* respectively. The method in *Step 4* is used to call mock list data and method in *Step 7* is used to call SharePoint lists from a SharePoint site.

In this step, we will write a `private` method will identify the environment and will render the list accordingly. Use the below code to add a private method in main web part file:

```
private _renderListAsync(): void {
  // Local environment
  if (Environment.type === EnvironmentType.Local) {
    this._getMockListData().then((response) => {
      this._renderList(response.value);
    });
  }
  else if (Environment.type == EnvironmentType.SharePoint ||
          Environment.type == EnvironmentType.
ClassicSharePoint) {
```

```
    this._getListData()
      .then((response) => {
        this._renderList(response.value);
      });
  }
}
```

In the above code, it's important to note that `Environment.type` property helps you to check if you are in a local or SharePoint environment and renders the respective method based on the environment.

12. In this step, we will modify the render method. Replace your render method with the following code and save the file:

```
this.domElement.innerHTML = `
  <div class="${ styles.helloWorld }">
    <div class="${ styles.container }">
      <div class="${ styles.row }">
        <div class="${ styles.column }">
          <span class="${ styles.title }">Welcome to
SharePoint!</span>
          <p class="${ styles.subTitle }">Customize SharePoint
experiences using web parts.</p>
          <p class="${ styles.description }">${escape(this.
properties.description)}</p>
          <p class="${ styles.description }">${escape(this.
properties.test)}</p>
          <p class="${ styles.description }">Loading from
${escape(this.context.pageContext.web.title)}</p>
          <a href="https://aka.ms/spfx" class="${ styles.button
}">
            <span class="${ styles.label }">Learn more</span>
          </a>
        </div>
      </div>
      <div id="spListContainer" />
    </div>
  </div>`;
```

```
this._renderListAsync();
```

Below is the screenshot of the modified render method:

```
public render(): void {
  this.domElement.innerHTML = `
    <div class="${ styles.helloWorld}">
      <div class="${ styles.container}">
        <div class="${ styles.row}">
          <div class="${ styles.column}">
            <span class="${ styles.title}">Welcome to SharePoint!</span>
            <p class="${ styles.subTitle}">Customize SharePoint experiences using Web Parts.</p>
            <p class="${ styles.description}">${escape(this.properties.description)}</p>
            <p class="${ styles.description }">Loading from ${escape(this.context.pageContext.web.title)}</p>
            <a href="https://aka.ms/spfx" class="${ styles.button}">
              <span class="${ styles.label}">Learn more</span>
            </a>
          </div>
        </div>
        <div id="spListContainer" />
      </div>
    </div>`;

  this._renderListAsync();
}
```

Figure 4.9

Output:

Since the `gulp serve` is running, we can directly navigate to the local workbench to check the output of the above steps.

Below is the output in the local workbench displaying the mock data:

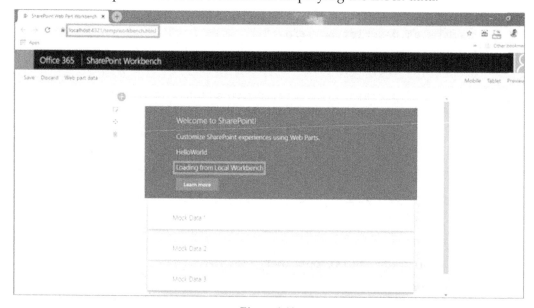

Figure 4.10

Below is the output in the SharePoint hosted workbench displaying the SharePoint lists present in a SharePoint new team site (You need to press *Enter* or refresh the SharePoint workbench to see the output):

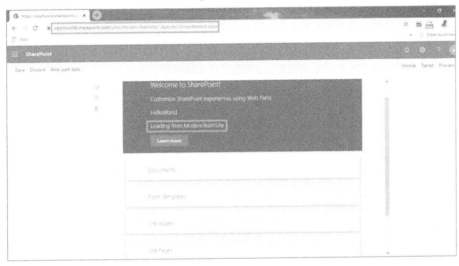

Figure 4.11

You can stop the `gulp serve` or terminate the gulp tasks using *Ctrl + C*.

Deploy web part on a SharePoint page

In this section, you will see how to package and deploy the SharePoint Framework web part on new SharePoint pages.

Below are the steps to package SharePoint Framework web part:

- The `package-solution.json` file defines the web part or packages metadata. The following screenshot is of `package-solution.json` file:

```
config > {} package-solution.json > ...
  1  {
  2    "$schema": "https://developer.microsoft.com/json-schemas/spfx-build/package-solution.schema.json",
  3    "solution": {
  4      "name": "firstspfx-webpart-client-side-solution",
  5      "id": "ade292cd-16db-4a10-9643-d2c53c8ab474",
  6      "version": "1.0.0.0",
  7      "includeClientSideAssets": true,
  8      "skipFeatureDeployment": true,
  9      "isDomainIsolated": false
 10    },
 11    "paths": {
 12      "zippedPackage": "solution/firstspfx-webpart.sppkg"
 13    }
 14  }
 15
```

Figure 4.12

In the console window (I am using node JS command prompt), enter the below command to package your client-side solution that contains the web part:

```
gulp package-solution
```

This command creates the package in the sharepoint | solution folder with the name firstspfx-webpart.sppkg, as shown in the following screenshot:

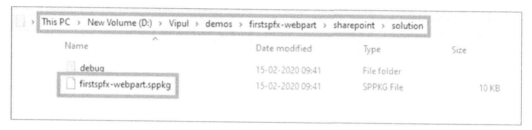

Figure 4.13

- Since we have packaged the web part, in this step, we will deploy the web part to the app catalog site collection of the tenant. (Refer steps for creating an app catalog in *Chapter 1*)

  Go to the app catalog site and upload or drag the firstspfx-webpart.sppkg in Apps for SharePoint library. The moment you upload the package file, a pop up (or dialog box) will open asking to deploy the package by trusting it, as shown in the following screenshot:

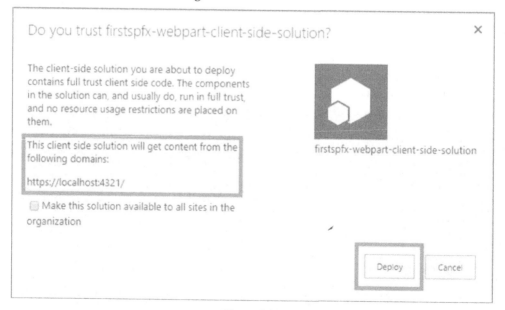

Figure 4.14

Select **Deploy**.

The following screenshot shows that the package has been added/uploaded successfully in the app catalog site, as the **App Package Error Message** column is not showing any error:

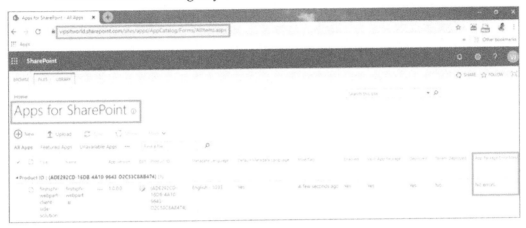

Figure 4.15

- Since the package has been uploaded to the app catalog site, it's time to add the app in the site collection (I created a new team site). Go to your site collection and add an app and select the **firstspfx-webpart-client-side-solution** app to install the app on the site, as shown in the following screenshot:

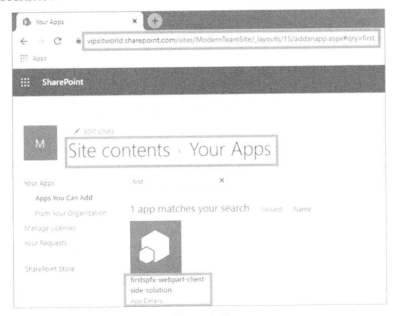

Figure 4.16

Select the app to add to your site (this will take a few seconds to add to your site). The site contents page will show your app once the installation will be completed, as shown in the following screenshot:

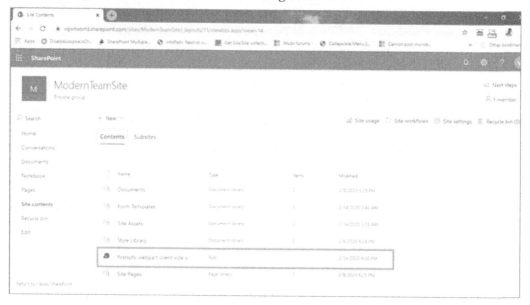

Figure 4.17

- Since you have deployed and installed the client-side solution in your site, in this step, we will add the web part on a SharePoint page. Before adding the web part to a SharePoint server-side page, make sure to run the local server using the below command. It is required because the web part resources like JavaScript and CSS files will be served from the local system:

```
gulp serve --nobrowser
```

`--nobrowser` is used in the above command because we don't want to launch SharePoint local workbench automatically.

- Add a page in your SharePoint site and add the firstspfx web part on to the page. You should see the web part developed in the previous section that retrieves all lists from the current site:

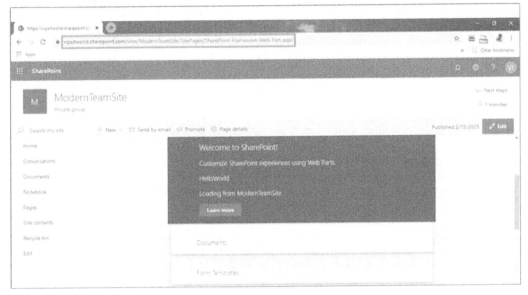

Figure 4.18

Configure SPFx web part icon

When SharePoint Framework web parts are added to a page, they display an icon and web part title. In this section of the chapter, we will see how we can change the SPFx web part icon.

By default, SPFx web part shows a default icon (Page type icon), as shown in the following screenshot:

Figure 4.19

In SPFx web part, in `manifest.json` file, there is a predefined entry for this icon, as shown in the following screenshot:

```
src > webparts > helloWorld > {} HelloWorldWebPart.manifest.json > ...
 1   {
 2     "$schema": "https://developer.microsoft.com/json-schemas/spfx/client-side-web-part-manifest.schema.json",
 3     "id": "67657205-7845-4b07-9429-42c733cb3b71",
 4     "alias": "HelloWorldWebPart",
 5     "componentType": "WebPart",
 6
 7     // The "*" signifies that the version should be taken from the package.json
 8     "version": "*",
 9     "manifestVersion": 2,
10
11     // If true, the component can only be installed on sites where Custom Script is allowed.
12     // Components that allow authors to embed arbitrary script code should set this to true.
13     // https://support.office.com/en-us/article/Turn-scripting-capabilities-on-or-off-1f2c515f-5d7e-448a-9fd7-835da
14     "requiresCustomScript": false,
15     "supportedHosts": ["SharePointWebPart"],
16
17     "preconfiguredEntries": [{
18       "groupId": "5c03119e-3074-46fd-976b-c60198311f70", // Other
19       "group": { "default": "Other" },
20       "title": { "default": "HelloWorld" },
21       "description": { "default": "HelloWorld description" },
22       "officeFabricIconFontName": "Page",
23       "properties": {
24         "description": "HelloWorld"
25       }
26     }]
27   }
```

Figure 4.20

Now we will see how we can change the default web part icon. There are three ways in which you can change the default icon.

Using Office UI Fabric icon

Office UI Fabric provides many icons that can be used for the SPFx web part icon. The following URL is having a list of icons provided by Office UI Fabric **https://developer.microsoft.com/en-us/fabric#/styles/web/icons**.

I have used a different icon (Airplane) and added in `manifest.json` file, as shown in the following screenshot:

```
 7     "preconfiguredEntries": [{
 8       "groupId": "5c03119e-3074-46fd-976b-c60198311f70", // Other
 9       "group": { "default": "Other" },
10       "title": { "default": "HelloWorld" },
11       "description": { "default": "HelloWorld description" },
12       "officeFabricIconFontName": "Airplane",
13       "properties": {
14         "description": "HelloWorld"
15       }
16     }]
17   }
```

Figure 4.21

The following screenshot is the output of adding Office UI Fabric icon:

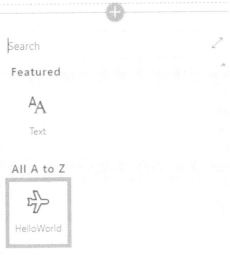

Figure 4.22

If the new icon is not displayed immediately in local workbench, then run the command: gulp clean and then again run the command: gulp serve to see the output in local workbench.

The following screenshot shows the gulp clean command in the console window:

```
Administrator: Node.js command prompt

D:\Vipul\demos\firstspfx-webpart>gulp clean
Build target: DEBUG
[11:11:22] Using gulpfile D:\Vipul\demos\firstspfx-webpart\gulpfile.js
[11:11:22] Starting gulp
[11:11:22] Starting 'clean'...
[11:11:22] Starting subtask 'clean'...
[11:11:22] Finished subtask 'clean' after 157 ms
[11:11:22] Finished 'clean' after 161 ms
[11:11:23] ===================[ Finished ]===================
[11:11:23] Project firstspfx-webpart version:0.0.1
[11:11:23] Build tools version:3.12.1
[11:11:23] Node version:v10.16.3
[11:11:23] Total duration:6.99 s
```

Figure 4.23

Using an external image

If you want to add a custom icon/image of your choice, then you will go ahead with this option. The external icon/image absolute URL needs to be specified in the "iconImageUrl" property, as shown in the following screenshot:

```
"preconfiguredEntries": [{
    "groupId": "5c03119e-3074-46fd-976b-c60198311f70",
    "group": { "default": "Other" },
    "title": { "default": "HelloWorld" },
    "description": { "default": "HelloWorld description" },
    "iconImageUrl": "https://sharepointeducation.files.wordpress.com/2017/09/vipul.jpg",
    "properties": {
        "description": "HelloWorld"
    }
}]
```

Figure 4.24

The following screenshot is the output of adding an external image:

Figure 4.25

Using a base64-encoded image

Instead of specifying the absolute URL of the custom image/icon, we can also use the base64 encoded image. There are many online services available to encode the images, and I have used the following URL to encode my custom image **https://www.base64-image.de/**.

Following is the screenshot of the encoded image and encoded string of the same image which I used in Point-2:

Figure 4.26

Once the image is encoded, copy the encoded string (by clicking on the copy to clipboard as shown in the above screenshot), and specify the encoded string in "iconImageUrl" property, as shown in the following screenshot:

```
"preconfiguredEntries": [{
  "groupId": "5c03119e-3074-46fd-976b-c60198311f70",
  "group": { "default": "Other" },
  "title": { "default": "HelloWorld" },
  "description": { "default": "HelloWorld description" },
  "iconImageUrl": "data:image/jpeg;base64,/9j/4AAQSkZJRgABAQAAAQABAAD/4QAqRXhpZgAASUkqAAgAAAABADEBAgAHAAAAGgAAA
  "properties": {
    "description": "HelloWorld"
  }
}]
```

Figure 4.27

If both "officeFabricIconFontName" and "iconImageUrl" properties are specified in the manifest file, then the icon specified in the "officeFabricIconFontName" property will take the preference and will be shown as web part icon.

Conclusion

In this chapter, we discussed how to access page context and test your first SPFx web part on local and SharePoint workbench. We also discussed deploying and installing the SPFx web part in a SharePoint site and adding the web part on the new

SharePoint page. Finally, we saw how you change the web part icon of a SharePoint Framework web part.

Points to remember

- SharePoint workbench page context provides properties such as web absolute and relative URL, web title, and user sign-in name.
- The two classes Environment and the `EnvironmentType` allow you to decide the environment; that is, the web part is running in the local workbench or SharePoint workbench.

Multiple Choice Questions

1. What is the extension of SharePoint Framework solution package?

    a. .sppkg

    b. .app

    c. .apk

    d. .apa

2. In which folder SharePoint Framework solution package gets created:

    a. /lib

    b. /sharepoint/solution

    c. /dist

    d. /temp

Answer

1. A
2. B

Questions

1. What is the command to package the SharePoint Framework web part solution?

2. What are the three ways in which you can configure the SPFx web part icon?

Key terms

- **SPHttpClient class:** This class helps to access SharePoint objects using REST APIs.

CHAPTER 5

Working with SPFx Web Part Property Pane

Web parts in classic SharePoint were configured using web part properties. In modern SharePoint or specifically SharePoint Framework, they are called property panes. The property panes allow controlling behavior and appearance of a web part on a new SharePoint page. In this chapter, we will deep dive into configuring property panes.

Structure

In this chapter, we will cover the following topics:

- Understanding property pane metadata
- SPFx solution for Property Pane
- Test the Property Pane in Local Workbench

Objective

After studying this chapter, you should be able to:

- Understand supported property fields
- Configure SPFx web part property pane

Understanding Property pane metadata

Property pane has three primary metadata:

- **Pages:** Allows you to separate complex interactions and divide the property pane across one or multiple pages. Pages contain a header and groups as metadata.
- **Header:** Defines the title of the property pane.
- **Groups:** This contains different property fields. Below is the list of out-of-the-box available property fields:

S.No.	Property Field	SPFx Typed Object
1.	Label	`PropertyPaneLabel`
2.	Button	`PropertyPaneButton`
3.	Checkbox	`PropertyPaneCheckbox`
4.	Dropdown	`PropertyPaneDropdown`
5.	Horizontal rule	`PropertyPaneHorizontalRule`
6.	Choice group	`PropertyPaneChoiceGroup`
7.	Link	`PropertyPaneLink`
8.	Slider	`PropertyPaneSlider`
9.	Textbox	`PropertyPaneTextField`
10.	Multi-line Textbox	`PropertyPaneTextField`
11.	Toggle	`PropertyPaneToggle`
12.	Custom	It is a custom implementation of property pane using a combination of the above types of objects

Table: 5.1

SPFx solution for Property pane

In this section, we will create an SPFx solution to test the web part property pane functionality. Follow the below steps for creating the solution.

1. Create a directory for SPFx solution using the below command:

   ```
   md spfxpropertypane
   ```

2. Navigate to the directory created in *Step 1* using the below command:

   ```
   cd spfxpropertypane
   ```

3. Use the following command to run the Yeoman SharePoint Generator to create the solution:

   ```
   yo @microsoft/sharepoint
   ```

4. Provide below values in the Yeoman generator wizard:

- **Solution Name:** Select default value by pressing enter
- **The target for the component:** SharePoint Online only (latest)
- **Place of files:** Current folder
- **Deployment option: N** to install on each site explicitly
- **Permission to access Web APIs: N** to do not grant permission to access Web API
- **Type of client-side component to create:** WebPart
- **Web Part name:** spfxpropertypane
- **Web part description:** Select default value by pressing *Enter*
- **A framework to use:** No JavaScript Framework

5. Once the Yeoman generator finishes generating the solution, open the solution in Visual Studio Code editor using `code .` command.

6. Open the file `SpfxpropertypaneWebPart.ts` located at located at \ `src\webparts\spfxPropertyPane`. Below is the screenshot of the default `getPropertyPaneConfiguration()` method, which contains the configurations to build the property pane:

```
protected getPropertyPaneConfiguration(): IPropertyPaneConfiguration {
  return {
    pages: [
      {
        header: {
          description: strings.PropertyPaneDescription
        },
        groups: [
          {
            groupName: strings.BasicGroupName,
            groupFields: [
              PropertyPaneTextField('description', {
                label: strings.DescriptionFieldLabel
              })
            ]
          }
        ]
      }
    ]
  };
}
```

Figure 5.1

The default class, `SpfxPropertyPaneWebPart`, accepts property type of interface `ISpfxPropertyPaneWebPartProps`, which, by default, has description property of type `string`. Below is the image showing default class implementing the interface `ISpfxpropertypaneWebPartProps`:

```
export interface ISpfxpropertypaneWebPartProps {
  description: string;
}

export default class SpfxpropertypaneWebPart extends BaseClientSideWebPart <ISpfxpropertypaneWebPartProps> {

  public render(): void {
    this.domElement.innerHTML = `
      <div class="${ styles.spfxpropertypane }">
        <div class="${ styles.container }">
          <div class="${ styles.row }">
            <div class="${ styles.column }">
              <span class="${ styles.title }">Welcome to SharePoint!</span>
              <p class="${ styles.subTitle }">Customize SharePoint experiences using Web Parts.</p>
              <p class="${ styles.description }">${escape(this.properties.description)}</p>
              <a href="https://aka.ms/spfx" class="${ styles.button }">
                <span class="${ styles.label }">Learn more</span>
              </a>
            </div>
          </div>
        </div>
      </div>`;
  }
}
```

Figure 5.2

The `import` section has the default properties defined, as shown in the below screenshot:

```
TS SpfxpropertypaneWebPart.ts ×

src > webparts > spfxpropertypane > TS SpfxpropertypaneWebPart.ts > ✿ SpfxpropertypaneWebPart > ⊙ render
1    import { Version } from '@microsoft/sp-core-library';
2    import {
3      IPropertyPaneConfiguration,
4      PropertyPaneTextField
5    } from '@microsoft/sp-property-pane';
6    import { BaseClientSideWebPart } from '@microsoft/sp-webpart-base';
7    import { escape } from '@microsoft/sp-lodash-subset';
```

Figure 5.3

7. In this step, we will add some properties and map to respective typed objects in the `getPropertyPaneConfiguration` method. Add the following code in `import` section to add the properties:

```
import {

    IPropertyPaneConfiguration,

    PropertyPaneTextField,
```

```
    PropertyPaneCheckbox,

    PropertyPaneDropdown,

    PropertyPaneToggle

} from '@microsoft/sp-property-pane';
```

8. Map the above properties to typed objects. Use the following code to add in the interface ISpfxpropertypaneWebPartProps:

```
export interface ISpfxpropertypaneWebPartProps {

    description: string;

    textbox: string;

    checkbox: string;

    dropdown: string;

    toggle: string;

}
```

Following is the screenshot showing ISpfxpropertypaneWebPartProps interface:

```
export interface ISpfxpropertypaneWebPartProps {
    description: string;
    textbox: string;
    checkbox: string;
    dropdown: string;
    toggle: string;
}
```

Figure 5.4

9. Replace the getPropertyPaneConfiguration method with the following code, which adds the new property pane fields and maps them to their respective typed objects:

```
protected getPropertyPaneConfiguration():
IPropertyPaneConfiguration {

    return {

        pages: [

            {

                header: {

                    description: strings.PropertyPaneDescription

                },

                groups: [
```

```
                {
                  groupName: strings.BasicGroupName,
                  groupFields: [
                  PropertyPaneTextField('description', {
                    label: 'Description'
                  }),
                  PropertyPaneTextField('textbox', {
                    label: 'Multi-line Text Field',
                    multiline: true
                  }),
                  PropertyPaneCheckbox('checkbox', {
                    text: 'Checkbox'
                  }),
                  PropertyPaneDropdown('dropdown', {
                    label: 'Dropdown',
                    options: [
                      { key: '1', text: 'One' },
                      { key: '2', text: 'Two' },
                      { key: '3', text: 'Three' },
                      { key: '4', text: 'Four' }
                    ]}),
                  PropertyPaneToggle('toggle', {
                    label: 'Toggle',
                    onText: 'On',
                    offText: 'Off'
                  })
                  ]
                }
              ]
            }
          ]
        };
      }
```

10. Modify the render() method, as shown below, to show the selected field values on the web part:

```
public render(): void {
  this.domElement.innerHTML = `
    <div class="${ styles.spfxpropertypane }">
      <div class="${ styles.container }">
        <div class="${ styles.row }">
          <div class="${ styles.column }">
            <span class="${ styles.title }">Welcome to SharePoint!</span>
            <p class="${ styles.subTitle }">Customize SharePoint experiences using Web Parts.</p>
            <p class="${ styles.description }">Description : ${escape(this.properties.description)}</p>

            <p class="${ styles.description }">Textbox : ${escape(this.properties.textbox)}</p>
            <p class="${ styles.description }">Checkbox : ${escape(this.properties.checkbox)}</p>
            <p class="${ styles.description }">Dropdown : ${escape(this.properties.dropdown)}</p>
            <p class="${ styles.description }">Toggle : ${escape(this.properties.toggle)}</p>

            <a href="https://aka.ms/spfx" class="${ styles.button }">
              <span class="${ styles.label }">Learn more</span>
            </a>
          </div>
        </div>
      </div>
    </div>`;
}
```

Figure 5.5

Test the Property pane in local workbench

In the command prompt, run the command gulp serve to test the web part property pane functionality. Add the web part on the local workbench as shown in below screenshot:

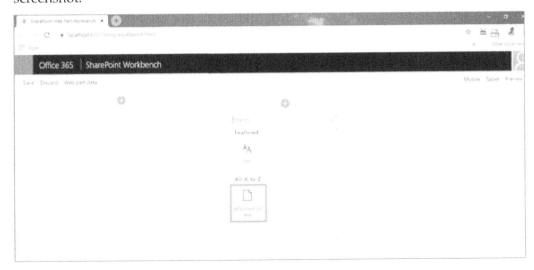

Figure 5.6

Below is the output showing a web part in which different properties are configured:

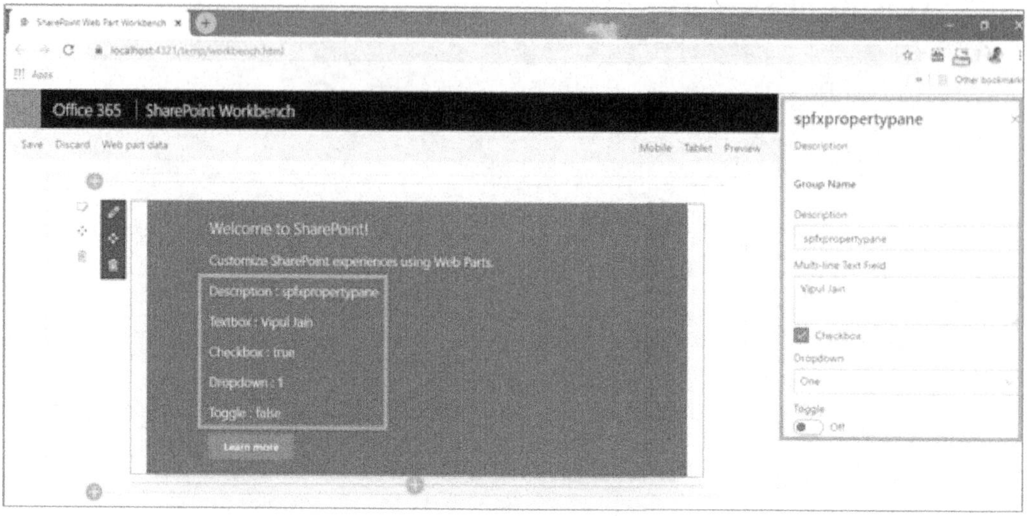

Figure 5.7

Conclusion

In this chapter, we discussed out-of-the-box available property fields and how we can use them in an SPFx web part solution. We can use predefined typed objects to create properties for the web part. In the next chapter, you will see different hosting options to deploy the SPFx client-side web part.

Points to remember

- All the properties should be mapped to respective typed objects.

Multiple Choice Question

1. In which method do we map all property pane fields to their respective typed objects?

    a. render() method

    b. OnInit() method

    c. getPropertyPaneConfiguration() method

    d. None of these

Answer

1. C

Questions

1. What are the three types of metadata in property pane?
2. What are the different property fields which can be used in the SPFx web part?

Key terms

- **Pages:** Allows you to separate complex interactions and divide the property pane across one or multiple pages. Pages contain a header and groups as metadata.

CHAPTER 6

Different Hosting Options for SPFx Web Part

In the previous chapters, we have seen that static assets are served from the local system or individually from the localhost. In this chapter, we will see different hosting options or environments where SPFx web parts can be served.

Structure

In this chapter, we will cover the following topics:

- Host client-side web part from Office 365 public CDN
- Host client-side web part from SharePoint Document Library
- Host client-side web part from Microsoft Azure CDN

Objective

After studying this chapter, you should be able to:

- Host SPFx web part from different hosting options
- Understand the importance of deploy-azure-storage.json file

Host client-side web part from Office 365 public CDN

In around April 2017, Microsoft announced and released Office 365 Public CDN for SharePoint. Please refer to the below URL for more information **https://developer. microsoft.com/en-us/office/blogs/general-availability-of-office-365-cdn/.**

Therefore, we can say that Office 365 **Content Delivery Network (CDN)** provides an easy way to host web part assets directly from your Office 365 tenant. Follow the below steps to enable CDN in your Office 365 tenant:

1. Download the latest version of SharePoint Online Management Shell from the below URL: **https://www.microsoft.com/en-us/download/details. aspx?id=35588.**

2. Open SharePoint Online Management Shell by running it as administrator.

3. Connect to your SharePoint Online tenant using below PowerShell command:

```
Connect-SPOService -Url https://<your-tenant-url>-admin.
sharepoint.com
```

The following screenshot shows the above command in SharePoint Online Management Shell:

Figure 6.1

4. A pop-up will open, asking for credentials. Enter the admin credentials to connect to SharePoint Online tenant, as shown in the following screenshot:

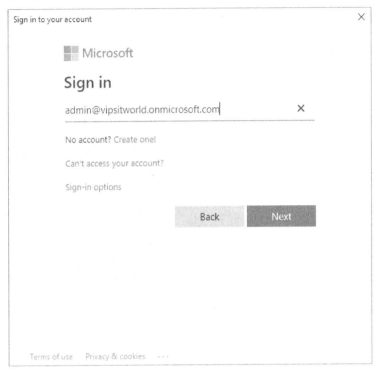

Figure 6.2

5. Run below PowerShell command to check the current status Office 365 public CDN settings in your tenant:

```
Get-SPOTenantCdnEnabled -CdnType Public
```

The above command will return the status of CDN. It will return True if CDN is enabled; otherwise, it will return False.

The following screenshot shows the result of the above command in my tenant:

Figure 6.3

```
Get-SPOTenantCdnOrigins -CdnType Public
```

The above command will return the location of already configured CDN origins. Since the CDN is not yet configured, in the first time, it will not return anything:

```
Get-SPOTenantCdnPolicies -CdnType Public
```

The above command will return the policy settings for CDN. The following screenshot shows the output of the above PowerShell command:

Figure 6.4

6. As shown in Figure 6.3, **SPOTenantCdnEnabled** property is **False**, so we need to enable this property or public CDN using the below PowerShell command:

```
Set-SPOTenantCdnEnabled -CdnType Public
```

7. Confirm settings by selecting **"Y"** and then press *Enter*. The following screenshot shows the output of running the PowerShell command given in *Step 6*.

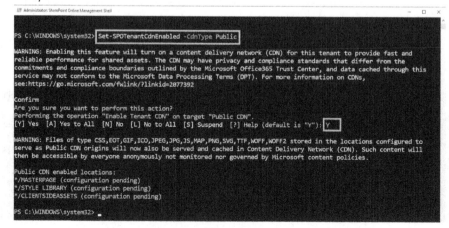

Figure 6.5

8. As shown in *Figure 6.5*, after enabling the CDN, */CLIENTSIDEASSETS origin is added by default as a valid origin. By default, allowed or supported file extensions are: CSS, EOT, GIF, ICO, JPEG, JPG, JS, MAP, PNG, SVG, TTF, and WOFF.

9. As shown in *Figure 6.5*, the configurations are pending; we can use the CDN only when the above locations are enabled. So, keep hitting the below command until all the locations are enabled (The configuration takes approximately 15 minutes to enable.):

Get-SPOTenantCdnEnabled -CdnType Public

The following screenshot shows that the CDN status in the tenant:

```
Administrator: SharePoint Online Management Shell
PS C:\WINDOWS\system32> Get-SPOTenantCdnEnabled -CdnType Public

Value
-----
True
```

Figure 6.6

The following screenshot shows that CDN origin is ready and none of the configurations are pending:

```
Administrator: SharePoint Online Management Shell
PS C:\WINDOWS\system32> Get-SPOTenantCdnOrigins -CdnType Public
*/MASTERPAGE
*/STYLE LIBRARY
*/CLIENTSIDEASSETS
PS C:\WINDOWS\system32>
```

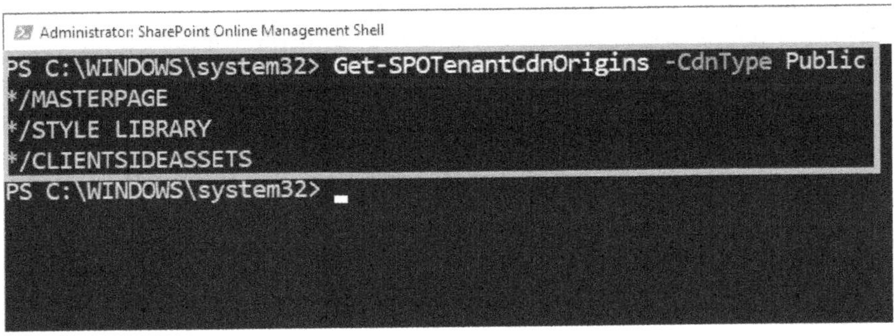

Figure 6.7

10. Open the SPFx web part solution in Visual Studio Code. Open package-solution.json file present in the config folder and make sure that "includeClientSideAssets" property is set to true.

The following screenshot shows the **package-solution.json** file which defines the package metadata and showing "**includeClientSideAssets**" property:

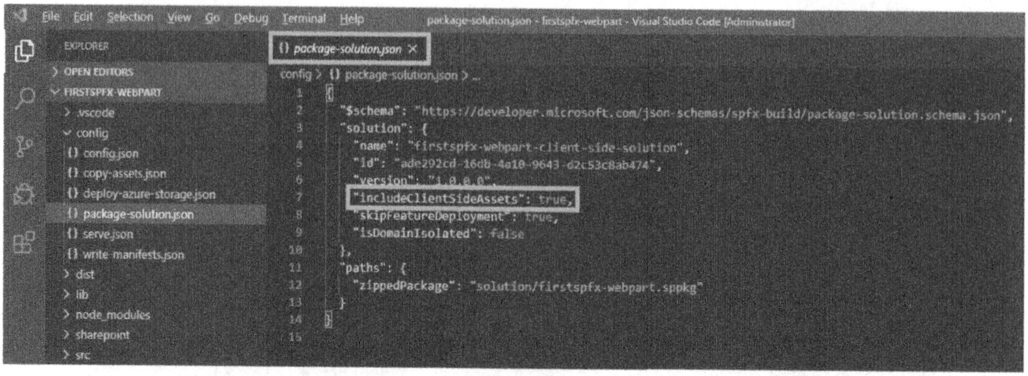

Figure 6.8

Deploy web part assets

Once CDN is enabled, and "**includeClientSideAssets**" is **true**, you are ready to package the solution. Follow the below steps to bundle and package the solution.

1. Run the below command in command prompt to bundle the solution:

   gulp bundle –ship

2. Run the below command to package the solution. These create (or updates the existing) .sppkg package in the solution folder:

   gulp package-solution –ship

   The following screenshot shows the updated .sppkg file after executing the above command:

Figure 6.9

3. Upload the newly created client-side solution package to the app catalog in your tenant.

4. The below screenshot shows that the domain list in the prompt says SharePoint Online. It is because the content is either served from the Office 365 CDN or the app catalog, depending on the tenant settings. Select **Deploy**:

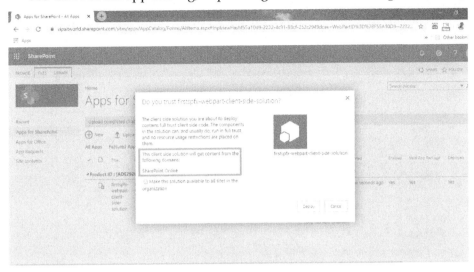

Figure 6.10

Test the web part

1. Add the web part to a SharePoint page and notice how the web part gets rendered even though node.js service is not running locally.

The following screenshot shows the output of adding the web part:

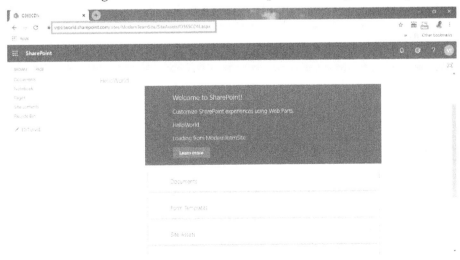

Figure 6.11

2. Select *F12* to open developer tools (tested in Google Chrome browser) and go to the **Sources** tab. Notice how the web part is getting loaded from the Public CDN URL.

Below is the image showing the web part is loaded from Public CDN URL:

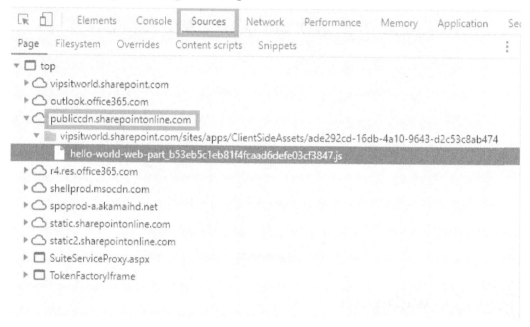

Figure 6.12

Host client-side web part from SharePoint Document Library

Below are the steps of deploying the SPFx webparts using the SharePoint library.

1. Create a new SharePoint Document Library in your SharePoint site. Below are the steps to create a new Document Library in SharePoint:

    -   Click **Settings** (gear icon) > **Add an App**
    -   Click **Document Library** tile
    -   Give it a name – **SPFxAssets**

2. The following screenshot shows the SharePoint Document library created using above steps:

Figure 6.13

3. Go to Library settings and click on **Permissions for this document library** and give read permission to all users. Added **Everyone except external users** group in the Site Visitors group. The following screenshot shows the Site Visitor group (Library inherited permissions from the site):

Figure 6.14

4. Create a new SPFx web part solution. Open the solution in Visual Studio Code. Open the `package-solution.json` file from the `config` folder.

Set `includeClientSideAssets` value as `false` (by default the value is `true`). The client-side assets will not be packaged inside the final package (`.sppkg` file) because these will be hosted in the SharePoint library.

The following screenshot shows the `package-solution.json` file:

Figure 6.15

5. Open `write-manifests.json` from the `config` folder. Update the CDN base path with SharePoint Library URL.

The following screenshot shows the `write-manifests.json` file with the updated `"cdnBasePath"`:

Figure 6.16

6. Prepare the package by typing the command: `gulp bundle -ship` in the command prompt. It will minimize the required assets to upload to CDN. The minified assets will be located at the `temp | deploy` folder.

The following screenshot shows the minified assets in `temp | deploy` folder:

Figure 6.17

7. Upload (or drag and drop) the files from `temp | deploy` folder to the SharePoint Document Library.

The following screenshot shows the SharePoint Document Library with minified assets:

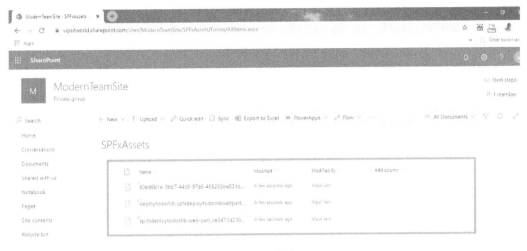

Figure 6.18

8. Deploy the package to SharePoint using the command: `gulp package-solution --ship`. It will create the solution package (.sppkg) in the `sharepoint | solution` folder.

9. Upload the package to SharePoint App Catalog and click **Deploy**.

Below is the screenshot showing URL is pointing to SharePoint Document Library:

Figure 6.19

10. Add the app on your site and then web part on a SharePoint page. Select *F12* to open developer tools (tested in Google Chrome browser) and go to the **Sources** tab. Notice how the web part is getting loaded from SharePoint Document Library.

Below is the screenshot showing the web part is loaded from SharePoint Document Library:

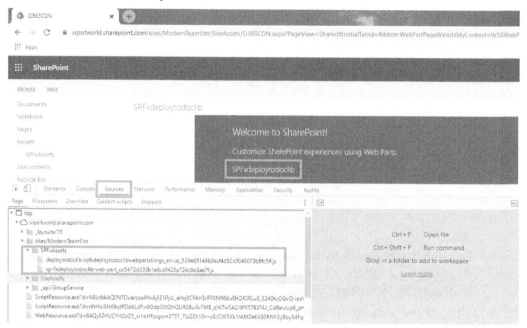

Figure 6.20

Quick tip

In *Step 4*, if you will use the Library URL as **https://vipsitworld.sharepoint.com/ sites/ModernTeamSite/SPFxAssets/forms/allitems.aspx** then you might encounter an error after adding web part on a SharePoint page. Hence, do not use `/forms/ allitems.aspx` while adding `cdnBasePath` URL in `write-manifests.json` file.

Below error might pop-up if you will use `/forms/allitems.aspx` in `cdnBasePath` URL:

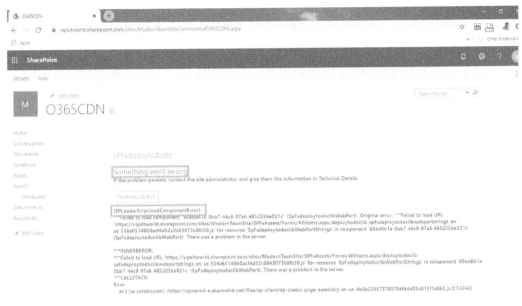

Figure 6.21

Host client-side web part from Microsoft Azure CDN

Below are the steps to Configure an Azure storage account:

1. Firstly, you need to configure an Azure storage account to deploy the SPFx web part to Azure. Log in to the Microsoft Azure portal using the below URL: **https://portal.azure.com/**.

2. Click on **Create a resource**, as shown in below screenshot:

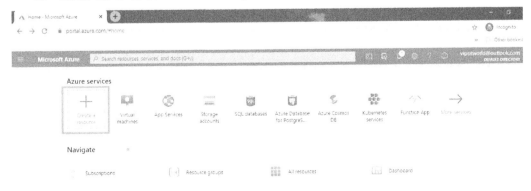

Figure 6.22

3. Click on **Storage account - blob, file, table, queue**, as shown in below screenshot:

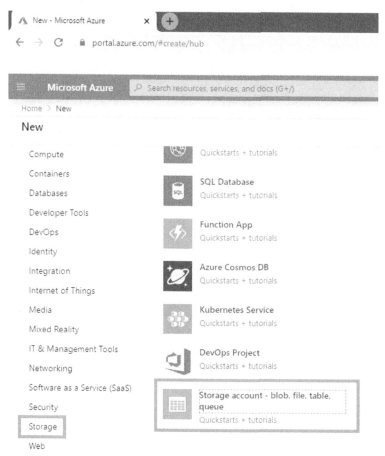

Figure 6.23

4. On the next screen, a form will open, asking to create a storage account. You need to fill two sections in this form, that is, **Project details** and **Instance details.**

Fill the details (**Subscription** and **Resource group**) of **Project details** section, as shown in the below screenshot:

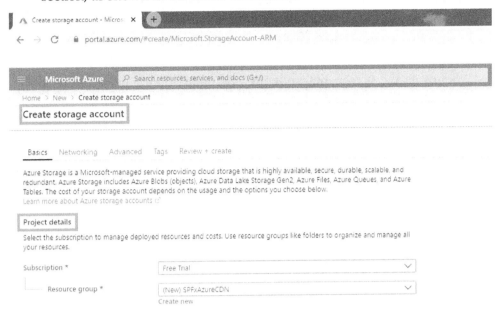

Figure 6.24

You can either choose an existing Resource group or can Create new.

Fill the details of **Instance details** section, as shown in the following screenshot:

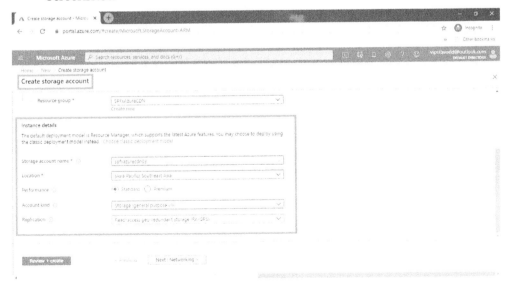

Figure 6.25

In Figure 6.25, the `Storage account` name field can contain only lowercase letters and numbers. Name must be between 3 and 24 characters

5. Click on the **Review + Create** button. Azure will take a few seconds to deploy the storage account to the specified Resource group.

   Below is the screenshot showing successful deployment to the resource group:

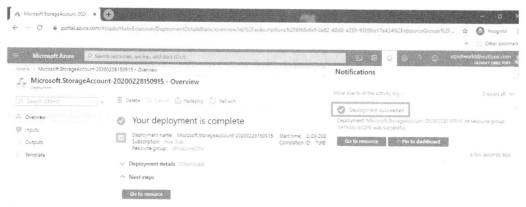

Figure 6.26

Below is the screenshot showing storage account in Resource group:

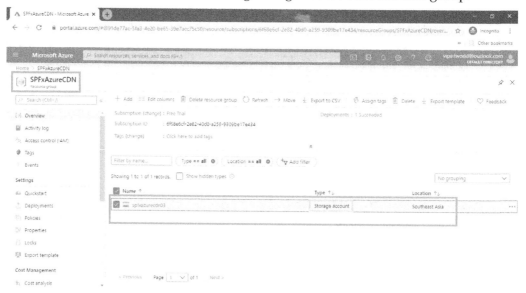

Figure 6.27

6. Click on the storage account name and then click on **Containers** from the storage account dashboard, as shown in below screenshot:

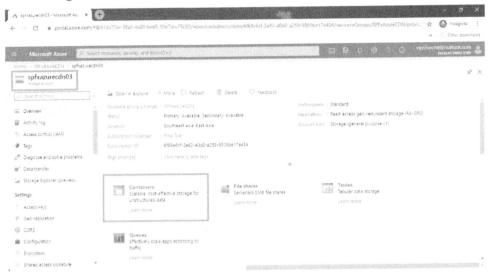

Figure 6.28

7. Select the **+ Container** and create a new container, as shown in the below screenshot:

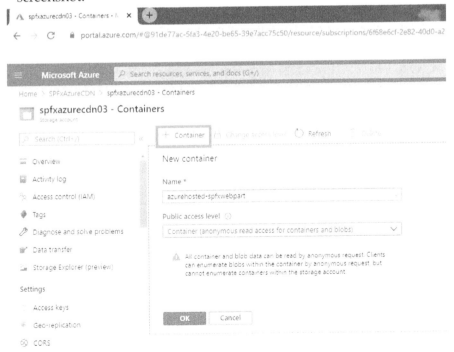

Figure 6.29

Click on **OK**, and a new container will be created.

8. In the storage account dashboard, select **Access keys**, and copy one of the access keys (to be used later), as shown in the following screenshot:

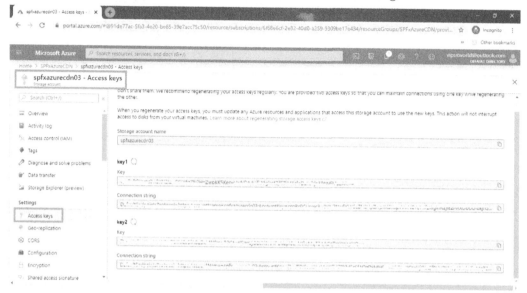

Figure 6.30

9. Select storage account from the dashboard and **Under BLOB Service**, select **Azure CDN**.

Create a new Azure CDN endpoint, as shown in the following screenshot:

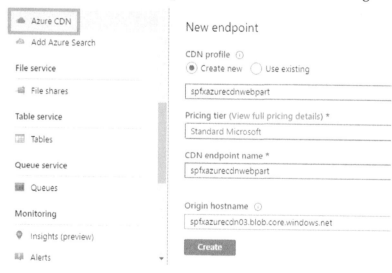

Figure 6.31

10. The created endpoint will appear in the endpoint list, as shown in the below screenshot:

Figure 6.32

Below are the steps to deploy SPFx web part to Azure CDN:

1. Create a new SPFx web part solution. Open the solution in Visual Studio Code. Open the `package-solution.json` file from the **config** folder. This file takes care of solution packaging.

   Set `includeClientSideAssets` value as `false` (by default the value is `true`). The client-side assets will not be packaged inside the final package (`.sppkg` file) because these assets will be hosted in the SharePoint library.

   The following screenshot shows the `package-solution.json` file:

Figure 6.33

In *Figure 6.33*, you need to add a property in the `package-solution.json` file name as `skipFeatureDeployment` and its value as true if you have answered the `tenant-scope` deployment option to be 'y' in a while scaffolding the solution using the Yeoman.

2. Open `deploy-azure-storage.json` file from the `config` folder to specify the Azure storage account details (storage account name, container name, and storage account accessKey), as shown in the following screenshot:

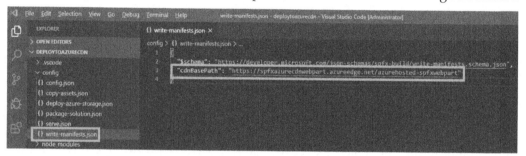

Figure 6.34

3. Open the `write-manifests.json` file from config folder to update the CDN base path as BLOB container endpoint, as shown in the following screenshot:

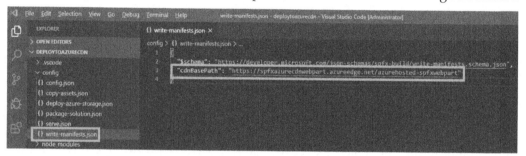

Figure 6.35

The CDN base path is the combination of CDN endpoints with the BLOB container.

4. In the command prompt, type the below command to prepare the package:

`gulp bundle –ship`

5. In the command prompt, type the below command to deploy the assets (JavaScript, CSS files) to Azure CDN:

`gulp deploy-azure-storage`

6. In the command prompt, type the below command to create the solution package (`.sppkg`) in `sharepoint | solution` folder:

`gulp package-solution –ship`

7. Upload the solution package (.sppkg) from sharepoint | solution folder to app catalog site and notice that the URL points to Azure CDN, as shown in below screenshot:

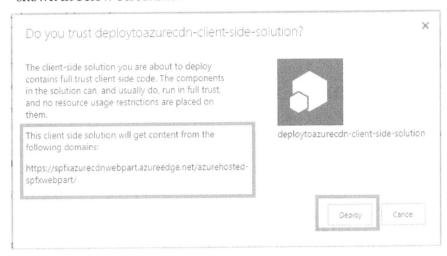

Figure 6.36

8. Click **Deploy**.

9. Add the app on your site and then web part on a SharePoint page. Select *F12* to open developer tools (tested in Google Chrome browser) and go to the **Sources** tab. Notice how the web part is getting loaded from Azure CDN.

Below is the screenshot showing the web part is loaded from Azure CDN:

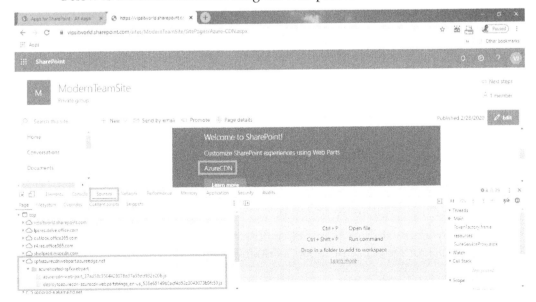

Figure 6.37

Conclusion

In this chapter, we discussed how the SharePoint framework provides out of box support to deploy assets to Office 365 CDN, SharePoint Document Library, and Azure CDN. In the next chapter, we will discuss implementing CRUD operation in SPFx with different JavaScript frameworks.

Points to remember

- Set `includeClientSideAssets` value as `false` (by default, the value is true) for deploying SPFx web parts in SharePoint Document Library and Azure CDN. The client-side assets will not be packaged in the final package (`.sppkg file`) because these assets will be hosted in the SharePoint library or Azure CDN.

Multiple Choice Question

1. In which file CDN Base Path is specified?

    a.   copy-assets.json

    b.   deploy-azure-storage.json

    c.   write-manifests.json

    d.   config.json

Answer

1. C

Questions

1. What are the three ways to host SharePoint Framework client-side web parts?

2. List the steps to configure an Azure storage account to deploy the SPFx web part.

Key terms

- **CDN:** Content Delivery Network

- **deploy-azure-storage.json:** This file contains the Azure storage account details, storage account name, container name, and storage account access key.

CHAPTER 7
CRUD Operations with Different JavaScript Frameworks

In the previous chapters, we have seen that how client-side web parts can be developed in SharePoint Framework; however, those web parts didn't interact with SharePoint objects. In this chapter, we will see how to interact with the SharePoint list for CRUD (Create, Read, Update, and Delete) operations using No JavaScript framework and React JS. The CRUD operations will be performed using REST APIs.

Structure

In this chapter, we will cover the following topics:

- CRUD operations using No JavaScript Framework
- Overview of React JS
- CRUD operations using React JS

Objective

After studying this chapter, you should be able to:

- Create models for list items
- Implement create, read, update and delete operations using No JavaScript Framework

- Understand the concepts of React JS
- Implement create, read, update and delete operations using React JS

CRUD operations using No JavaScript Framework

Below are the steps to create an SPFx solution for implementing CRUD operations using No JavaScript Framework:

1. Create a directory for SPFx solution using the below command:

   `md spfx-crud-nojavascriptframework`

2. Navigate to the directory created in Step 1 using the below command:

   `cd spfx-crud-nojavascriptframework`

3. Use the below command to run Yeoman SharePoint Generator to create the solution:

   `yo @microsoft/sharepoint`

4. Provide below values in the Yeoman generator wizard:
   - **Solution Name:** Select default value by pressing *Enter*
   - **Target for the component:** SharePoint Online only (latest)
   - **Place of files:** Current folder
   - **Deployment option:** *N* to install on each site explicitly
   - **Permission to access Web APIs:** *N* to avoid granting permissions to access Web APIs
   - **Type of client-side component to create:** WebPart
   - **Web part name:** CRUDNoFramework
   - **Web part description:** Select default value by pressing *Enter*
   - **The framework to use:** No JavaScript Framework

5. Once the Yeoman generator finishes generating the solution, open the solution in Visual Studio Code editor using `code .` command.

6. Change the description property (which is available by default) to list name property so that property for list name can be configured. This property will be used to configure the list name (in web part property pane) on which the CRUD operations will be performed.

   Open `mystrings.d.ts` file located under `src` | `webparts` | `crudNoFramework` | `loc` folder and rename `DescriptionFieldLabel` (by default) to `ListNameFieldLabel`.

The following screenshot shows the `mystrings.d.ts` file:

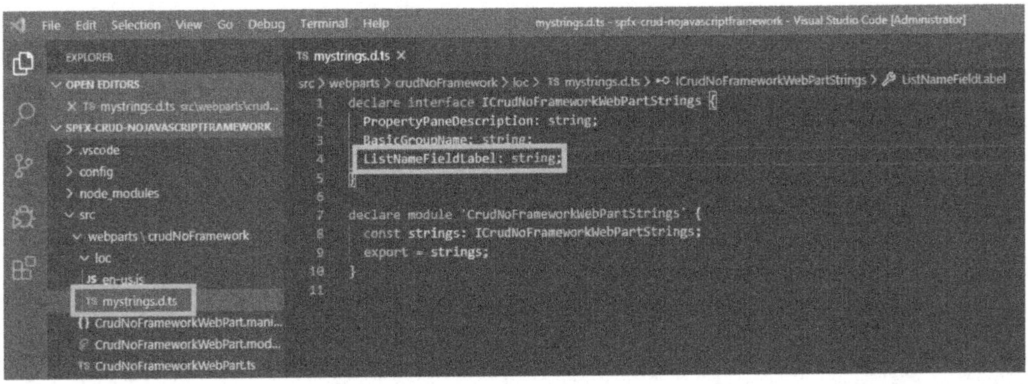

Figure 7.1

7. Open `en-us.js` file located under `src | webparts | crudNoFramework | loc` folder and set the display name for `listName` property, as shown in the following screenshot:

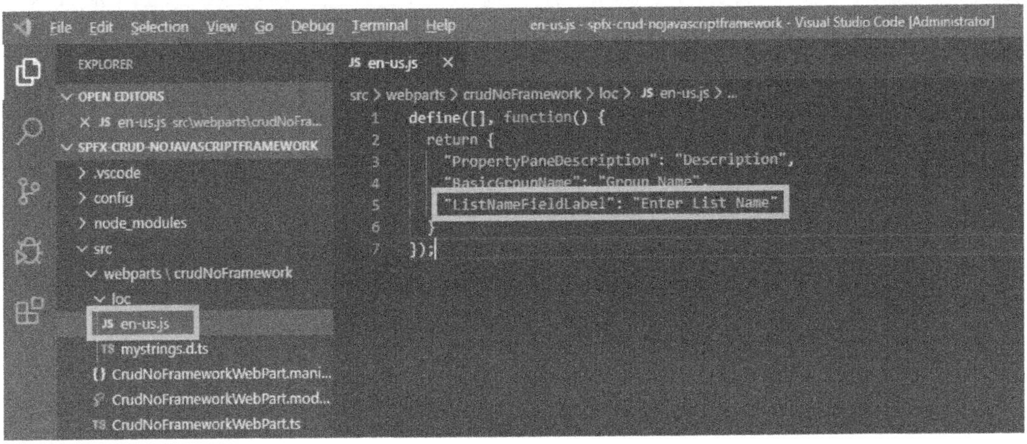

Figure 7.2

8. Open `CrudNoFrameworkWebPart.ts` file located under `src | webparts | crudNoFramework` folder and rename description property pane field to `listName`. You need to make changes at three places in this file, that is, in

the interface, in render() method and getPropertyPaneConfiguration() method, as shown in the following screenshot:

```
TS CrudNoFrameworkWebPart.ts ×
src > webparts > crudNoFramework > TS CrudNoFrameworkWebPart.ts > ⚡ CrudNoFrameworkWebPart > ⊕ render
12   export interface ICrudNoFrameworkWebPartProps {
13     listName: string;
14   }
15
16   export default class CrudNoFrameworkWebPart extends BaseClientSideWebPart <ICrudNoFrameworkWebPartProps> {
17
18   public render(): void {
19     this.domElement.innerHTML = `
20       <div class="${ styles.crudNoFramework }">
21         <div class="${ styles.container }">
22           <div class="${ styles.row }">
23             <div class="${ styles.column }">
24               <span class="${ styles.title }">Welcome to SharePoint!</span>
25               <p class="${ styles.subTitle }">Customize SharePoint experiences using Web Parts.</p>
26               <p class="${ styles.description }">${escape(this.properties.listName)}</p>
27               <a href="https://aka.ms/spfx" class="${ styles.button }">
28                 <span class="${ styles.label }">Learn more</span>
29               </a>
30             </div>
31           </div>
32         </div>
33       </div>`;
34   }
```

Figure 7.3

The following screenshot shows the changes required in getPropertyPaneConfiguration() method:

```
protected getPropertyPaneConfiguration(): IPropertyPaneConfiguration {
  return {
    pages: [
      {
        header: {
          description: strings.PropertyPaneDescription
        },
        groups: [
          {
            groupName: strings.BasicGroupName,
            groupFields: [
              PropertyPaneTextField('listName', {
                label: strings.ListNameFieldLabel
              })
            ]
          }
        ]
      }
    ]
  };
}
```

Figure 7.4

9. In the console window (or command prompt, run the below command) to test the web part in local workbench:

    ```
    gulp serve
    ```

10. The following screenshots show that `listName` property is getting reflected in web part property pane:

Figure 7.5

11. In this step, we will create a model for the list item. Let's add a new class (`IListItem.ts`), which will represent the list item. As shown in the below screenshot, we have added two properties of the list item, that is, `Title` and `Id`:

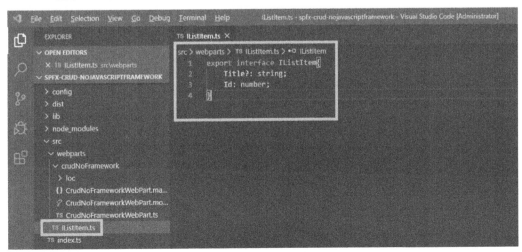

Figure 7.6

12. Open `CrudNoFrameworkWebPart.ts` file located under `src | webparts | crudNoFramework` folder and modify the `render()` method by adding buttons for CRUD operations and also add event handlers for each of these buttons.

Below is the screenshot showing the modified `render()` method with creating, read, update, and delete buttons added along with event handler (`setEventHandlers`):

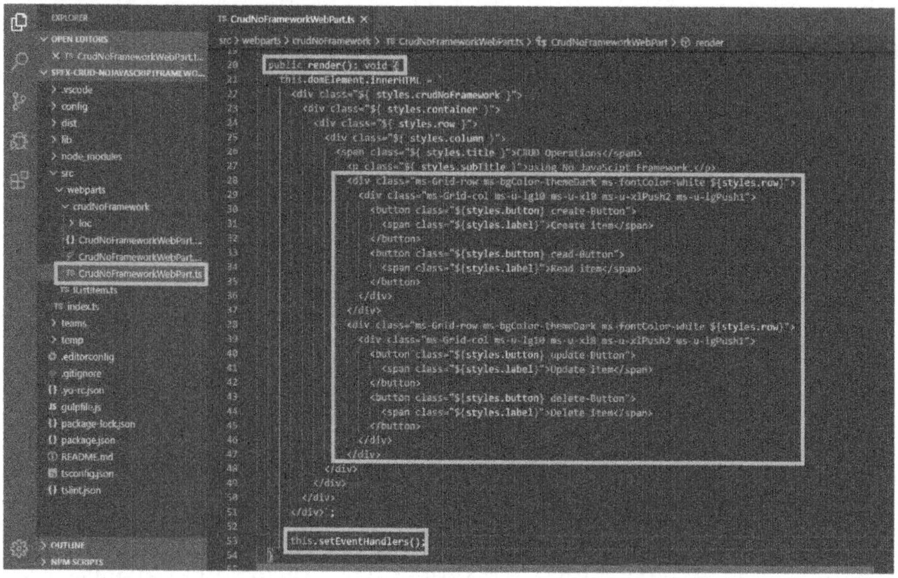

Figure 7.7

13. Now, we will define the body of the `setEventHandlers()` event handler, which will call different methods to implement CRUD operations.

Below is the screenshot showing event handler calling different CRUD operations methods:

```
private setEventHandlers(): void {
    const webPart: CrudNoFrameworkWebPart = this;
    this.domElement.querySelector('button.create-Button').addEventListener('click', () => { webPart.createItem(); });
    this.domElement.querySelector('button.read-Button').addEventListener('click', () => { webPart.readItem(); });
    this.domElement.querySelector('button.update-Button').addEventListener('click', () => { webPart.updateItem(); });
    this.domElement.querySelector('button.delete-Button').addEventListener('click', () => { webPart.deleteItem(); });
}

private createItem(): void{

}

private readItem(): void{

}

private updateItem(): void{

}

private deleteItem(): void{

}
```

Figure 7.8

14. In the command prompt type, `gulp serve` to see the buttons in webpart on the local workbench.

    Below is the screenshot showing buttons added in the web part on the local workbench:

Figure 7.9

15. The CRUD operations will be performed on the latest item of the SharePoint list. Below is a generic method implemented to return the ID of the latest item from the list. We will use the REST API to query the latest item ID of the list.

    Below is the REST API URL used in this method:

```
/_api/web/lists/getbytitle('${this.properties.listName}')/
items?$orderby=Id desc&$top=1&$select=id
```

Below is the screenshot showing a generic method to get the latest item ID of a SharePoint list:

```
private getLatestItemId(): Promise<number> {
    return new Promise<number>((resolve: (itemId: number) => void, reject: (error: any) => void): void => {
        this.context.spHttpClient.get(`${this.context.pageContext.web.absoluteUrl}/_api/web/lists/getbytitle('${this.properties.listName}')/items?
        $orderby=Id desc&$top=1&$select=Id`,
        SPHttpClient.configurations.v1,
        {
            headers: [
            'Accept': 'application/json;odata=nometadata',
            'odata-version': ''
            ]
        })
        .then((response: SPHttpClientResponse): Promise<{ value: { Id: number }[] }> => {
            return response.json();
        }, (error: any): void => {
            reject(error);
        })
        .then((response: { value: { Id: number }[] }): void => {
            if (response.value.length === 0) {
                resolve(-1);
            }
            else {
                resolve(response.value[0].Id);
            }
        });
    });
}
```

Figure 7.10

Before adding the above generic method, add the below import **statement to call** SPHttpClient **and** SPHttpClientResponse **classes:**

```
import { SPHttpClient, SPHttpClientResponse } from '@microsoft/sp-http';
```

16. From this step, we will start implementing CRUD operations. In this step, we will implement the **createItem()** method, which will create a new item in the SharePoint list.

    Below is the REST API URL used in this method:

    ```
    /_api/web/lists/getbytitle('${this.properties.listName}')/items
    ```

    Below is the screenshot showing code of **createItem()** method in which REST API is used to create a new item in the SharePoint list:

```
private createItem(): void{
  this.updateStatus('Creating item...');
  this.getListItemEntityTypeName()
    .then((listItemEntityTypeName: string): Promise<SPHttpClientResponse> => {
      const body: string = JSON.stringify({
        '__metadata': {
          'type': listItemEntityTypeName
        },
        'Title': `Item ${new Date()}`
      });
      return this.context.spHttpClient.post(`${this.context.pageContext.web.absoluteUrl}/_api/web/lists/getbytitle('${this.properties.listName}')/items`,
        SPHttpClient.configurations.v1,
        {
          headers: {
            'Accept': 'application/json;odata=nometadata',
            'Content-type': 'application/json;odata=verbose',
            'odata-version': ''
          },
          body: body
        });
    })
    .then((response: SPHttpClientResponse): Promise<IListItem> => {
      return response.json();
    })
    .then((item: IListItem): void => {
      this.updateStatus(`Item '${item.Title}' (ID: ${item.Id}) successfully created`);
    }, (error: any): void => {
      this.updateStatus('Error while creating the item: ' + error);
    });
}
```

Figure 7.11

17. In this step, we will implement the `readItem()` method, which will read the latest item from a SharePoint list.

    Below is the REST API URL used in this method:

    ```
    /_api/web/lists/getbytitle('${this.properties.listName}')/
    items(${itemId})?$select=Title,Id
    ```

    Below is the screenshot showing code of `readItem()` method in which REST API is used to read the latest item from SharePoint list:

```
private readItem(): void{
  this.updateStatus('Loading latest items...');
  this.getLatestItemId()
    .then((itemId: number): Promise<SPHttpClientResponse> => {
      if (itemId === -1) {
        throw new Error('No items found in the list');
      }

      this.updateStatus(`Loading information about item ID: ${itemId}...`);
      return this.context.spHttpClient.get(`${this.context.pageContext.web.absoluteUrl}/_api/web/lists/getbytitle('${this.properties.listName}')`,
        SPHttpClient.configurations.v1,
        {
          headers: {
            'Accept': 'application/json;odata=nometadata',
            'odata-version': ''
          }
        });
    })
    .then((response: SPHttpClientResponse): Promise<IListItem> => {
      return response.json();
    })
    .then((item: IListItem): void => {
      this.updateStatus(`Item ID: ${item.Id}, Title: ${item.Title}`);
    }, (error: any): void => {
      this.updateStatus('Loading latest item failed with error: ' + error);
    });
}
```

Figure 7.12

18. In this step, we will implement the **updateItem()** method, which will update the latest item from a SharePoint list.

Below is the REST API URL used in this method for GET request:

```
/_api/web/lists/getbytitle('${this.properties.listName}')/
items(${latestItemId})?$select=Id
```

Below is the screenshot showing code of **updateItem()** method to get the latest item Id:

```
private updateItem(): void{
  this.updateStatus('Loading latest items...');
  let latestItemId: number = undefined;
  let etag: string = undefined;
  let listItemEntityTypeName: string = undefined;
  this.getListItemEntityTypeName()
    .then((listItemType: string): Promise<number> => {
      listItemEntityTypeName = listItemType;
      return this.getLatestItemId();
    })
    .then((itemId: number): Promise<SPHttpClientResponse> => {
      if (itemId === -1) {
        throw new Error('No items found in the list');
      }

      latestItemId = itemId;
      this.updateStatus(`Loading information about item ID: ${latestItemId}...`);
      return this.context.spHttpClient.get(`${this.context.pageContext.web.absoluteUrl}/_api/web/lists/getbytitle('${this.properties.listName}
        SPHttpClient.configurations.v1,
        {
          headers: {
            'Accept': 'application/json;odata=nometadata',
            'odata-version': ''
          }
        });
    })
    .then((response: SPHttpClientResponse): Promise<IListItem> => {
      etag = response.headers.get('ETag');
      return response.json();
    })
```

Figure 7.13

Below is the REST API URL used in this method for POST request:

```
/_api/web/lists/getbytitle('${this.properties.listName}')/
items(${item.Id})
```

Below is the screenshot showing code of `updateItem()` method to update the latest item:

```
.then((response: SPHttpClientResponse): Promise<IListItem> => {
  etag = response.headers.get('ETag');
  return response.json();
})
.then((item: IListItem): Promise<SPHttpClientResponse> => {
  this.updateStatus(`Updating item with ID: ${latestItemId}...`);
  const body: string = JSON.stringify({
    '__metadata': {
      'type': listItemEntityTypeName
    },
    'Title': `Item ${new Date()}`
  });
  return this.context.spHttpClient.post(`${this.context.pageContext.web.absoluteUrl}/_api/web/lists/getbytitle('${this.properties.listName}')`,
    SPHttpClient.configurations.v1,
    {
      headers: {
        'Accept': 'application/json;odata=nometadata',
        'Content-type': 'application/json;odata=verbose',
        'odata-version': '',
        'IF-MATCH': etag,
        'X-HTTP-Method': 'MERGE'
      },
      body: body
    });
})
.then((response: SPHttpClientResponse): void => {
  this.updateStatus(`Item with ID: ${latestItemId} successfully updated`);
}, (error: any): void => {
  this.updateStatus(`Error updating item: ${error}`);
});
}
```

Figure 7.14

For updating an item in the SharePoint list, you need first to get the item ID (GET operation), which needs to be updated and then update the item using POST operation. For both these operations, we can use REST API in the same method call.

19. In this step, we will implement `deleteItem()` method, which will delete the latest item from a SharePoint list.

   Below is the REST API URL used in this method for GET request:

   ```
   /_api/web/lists/getbytitle('${this.properties.listName}')/
   items(${latestItemId})?$select=Id
   ```

Below is the screenshot showing code of `deleteItem()` method in which REST API is used to read the latest item from SharePoint list:

```
private deleteItem(): void{
    if (!window.confirm('Are you sure you want to delete the latest item?')) {
        return;
    }

    this.updateStatus('Loading latest items...');
    let latestItemId: number = undefined;
    let etag: string = undefined;
    this.getLatestItemId()
        .then((itemId: number): Promise<SPHttpClientResponse> => {
            if (itemId === -1) {
                throw new Error('No items found in the list');
            }

            latestItemId = itemId;
            this.updateStatus(`Loading information about item ID: ${latestItemId}...`);
            return this.context.spHttpClient.get(`${this.context.pageContext.web.absoluteUrl}/_api/web/lists/getbytitle('${this.properties.listName}')
                SPHttpClient.configurations.v1,
                {
                    headers: {
                        'Accept': 'application/json;odata=nometadata',
                        'odata-version': ''
                    }
                });
        })
        .then((response: SPHttpClientResponse): Promise<IListItem> => {
            etag = response.headers.get('ETag');
            return response.json();
        })
```

Figure 7.15

Below is the REST API URL used in this method for POST request:

```
/_api/web/lists/getbytitle('${this.properties.listName}')/
items(${item.Id})
```

Below is the screenshot showing code of `deleteItem()` method in which REST API is used to delete the latest item from SharePoint list:

```
        .then((item: IListItem): Promise<SPHttpClientResponse> => {
            this.updateStatus(`Deleting item with ID: ${latestItemId}...`);
            return this.context.spHttpClient.post(`${this.context.pageContext.web.absoluteUrl}/_api/web/lists/getbytitle('${this.properties.listName}')
                SPHttpClient.configurations.v1,
                {
                    headers: {
                        'Accept': 'application/json;odata=nometadata',
                        'Content-type': 'application/json;odata=verbose',
                        'odata-version': '',
                        'IF-MATCH': etag,
                        'X-HTTP-Method': 'DELETE'
                    }
                });
        })
        .then((response: SPHttpClientResponse): void => {
            this.updateStatus(`Item with ID: ${latestItemId} successfully deleted`);
        }, (error: any): void => {
            this.updateStatus(`Error deleting item: ${error}`);
        });
    }
```

Figure 7.16

Although for Update and Delete operations, we have used the same REST API URL for GET and POST methods, note that 'X-HTTP-Method' value is different. For Update, the value is MERGE, and for the delete operation, its value is DELETE.

20. In the command prompt, type the command `gulp serve` to test the SPFx web part on SharePoint workbench (`<your-site-url>/_layouts/workbench. aspx`). Click on the buttons (**Create item, Read item, Update item, and Delete item)** to test the webpart and verify that the respective operations are taking place in a SharePoint list.

Below is the screenshot showing the list name specified in the property pane (`CRUDNoJavaScriptFramework`) and web part showing the message as **Ready**:

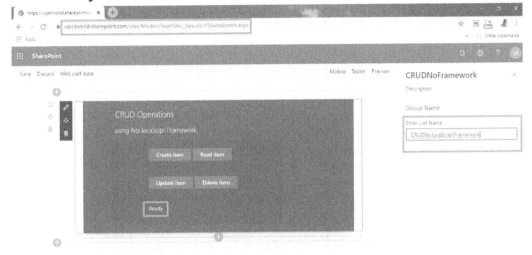

Figure 7.17

Below is the screenshot showing `Create item` operation in the web part:

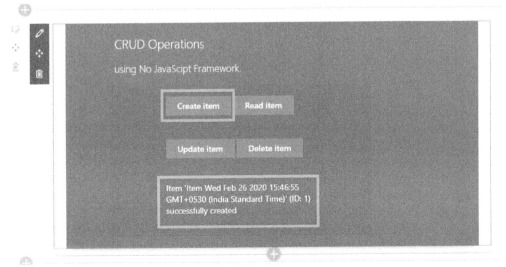

Figure 7.18

Below is the screenshot showing an item is created in a SharePoint list:

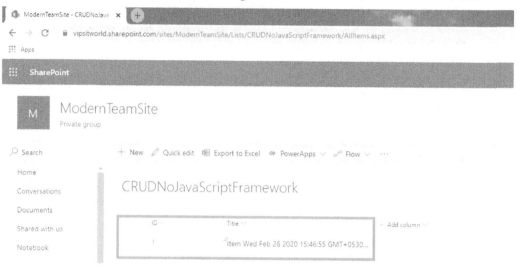

Figure 7.19

Below is the screenshot showing **Read item** operation in the web part:

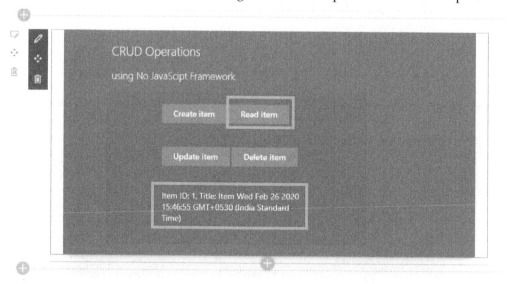

Figure 7.20

Below is the screenshot showing **Update item** operation in the web part:

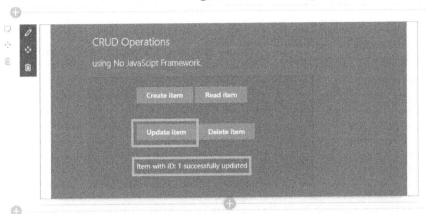

Figure 7.21

Below is the screenshot showing an alert when the **Delete item** button is clicked:

Figure 7.22

Below is the screenshot showing **Delete item** operation in the web part:

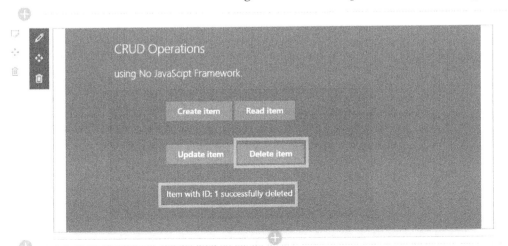

Figure 7.23

Overview of React JS

React JS is an open-source JavaScript library used to develop User Interfaces. React JS was introduced by Facebook in May 2013; however, it was open-sourced in March 2015. It is the View in the **MVC (Model-View-Controller)** model, as shown in the below screenshot:

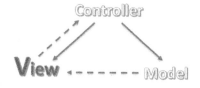

Figure 7.24

Concept of virtual DOM

React JS introduced a new concept called **Virtual DOM**. But before understanding this concept, let's find the problem with the traditional DOM. We know that Model gives data to View, which in turn creates a DOM for it. Now each time data is updated by the **Model**, and **View** had to create a new DOM for it. It puts a heavy load on **View** and makes application processing slower, which results in slow performing applications.

With ReactJS, when Model gives data to View, and if the DOM is empty, it will create a DOM for it. Now whenever the data updates, React will create a Virtual DOM for it and compare the current DOM with the previous one. Once the changes are calculated, it will update the Real DOM with only the elements that have changed. Hence, we can say that the Virtual DOM is the JavaScript object model that React uses to calculate user interface changes. By performing this calculation logically, React can free the developers from tracking individual UI changes.

React JS fundamentals

The following diagram displays the primary or core fundamentals of React JS:

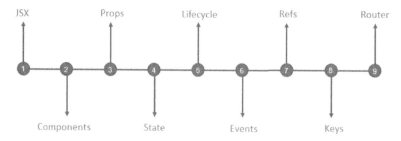

Figure 7.25

Below is a brief description of **JSX, Components, Props, State, and Lifecycle.**

JSX

JSX is a combination of HTML and JS. JSX stands for JavaScript XML. After compilation, JSX expressions become regular JavaScript function and corresponds to JavaScript objects.

Components and Props

Everything is React JS is a component. Components split the UI into independent, reusable pieces. Each component corresponds to an element in the DOM. Conceptually, components are like JavaScript functions. They accept arbitrary inputs (called **props**) and return React elements. You can define components in two ways – as a function component or as a Class component.

> Always start to React component names with a capital letter. For example, <div /> represents an HTML div tag, but <Employee /> represents a component.

Props are read-only components. Whether components are declared as function or class, it must never change its props. Such components are called **pure functions.**

> All React components must act like pure functions concerning their props.

State and Lifecycle

In addition to props, React components have another way of holding data called **State**. To use State, we have to use a class component. In the class constructor, we initialize the component state to a default value. The setState() method merges the new state with the old state.

> Never modify State directly, instead use the setState() method, and the only place where you can assign this.state is the constructor.

React provides various methods that notify when a certain stage of the lifecycle (mount or unmount) occurs, and these are called Lifecycle methods. These are special event handlers that are called at various points in components life.

The entire lifecycle of a React component is divided into four phases (starting from Initial Phase), as shown in the following diagram:

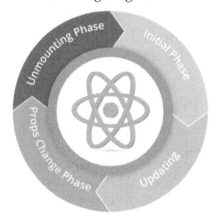

Figure 7.26

All these phases have different methods associated with it. The initial phase has two essential methods called componentDidMount() and componentWillUnmount().

The following table shows a comparison between the two methods:

ComponentWillMount()	ComponentDidMount()
This method is called immediately before the component is rendered and is used to assess props. It is called only once in the component lifecycle.	This method is called after the initial render of the component. In this method, we can call the setState() method to change the state of our application and render the updated data.

Table 7.1

Below is the order of events which happens typically in a component lifecycle:

1. componentWillMount() method will be called
2. The initial state is set in the constructor
3. render() method gets called
4. componentDidMount() method gets called
5. setState() method is called
6. Finally, again render() method is called, and the newly fetched data is displayed in the component

Advantages of React JS

- Application performance increases

- Can be used on the client as well as server-side
- Code readability gets improved
- It can be used easily with other frameworks like Angular etc

You can read more about React JS at https://reactjs.org/.

CRUD operations using React JS

Below are the steps to create an SPFx solution for implementing CRUD operations using React JS:

1. Create a directory for SPFx solution using the below command:

   md spfx-crud-ReactJS

2. Navigate to the directory created in Step 1 using the below command:

   cd spfx-crud-ReactJS

3. Use the below command to run Yeoman SharePoint Generator to create the solution:

   yo @microsoft/sharepoint

4. Provide below values in the Yeoman generator wizard:

   - **Solution Name:** Select default value by pressing *Enter*
   - **Target for the component:** SharePoint Online only (latest)
   - **Place of files:** Current folder
   - **Deployment option:** *N* to install on each site explicitly
   - **Permission to access Web APIs:** *N* to avoid granting permissions to access Web APIs
   - **Type of client-side component to create:** WebPart
   - **Web part name:** CRUDReactJS
   - **Web part description:** Select default value by pressing *Enter*
   - **The framework to use:** React

5. Once the Yeoman generator finishes generating the solution, open the solution in Visual Studio Code editor using code . command.

6. Change the description property (which is available by default) to list name property so that property for list name can be configured. This property will be used to configure the list name (in web part property pane) on which the CRUD operations will be performed.

   Open mystrings.d.ts file located under src | webparts | crudReactJs | loc folder and rename DescriptionFieldLabel (by default) to ListNameFieldLabel.

Below is the screenshot showing `mystrings.d.ts` file:

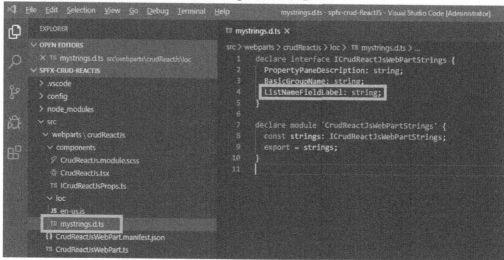

Figure 7.27

7. Open `en-us.js` file located under `src | webparts | crudReactJs | loc` folder and set the display name for `listName` property, as shown in the following screenshot:

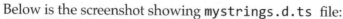

Figure 7.28

8. Open the interface file (`ICrudReactJsProps.ts`) located under `src |  webparts | crudReactJS | components` and set the member name to `listName`:

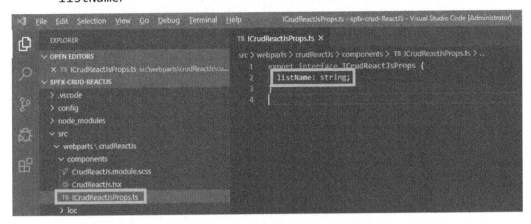

Figure 7.29

9. Open `CrudNoFrameworkWebPart.ts` file located under `src |  webparts | crudReactJs` folder and rename description property pane field to `listName`. You need to make changes at three places in this file, that is, in the interface, in `render()` method and `getPropertyPaneConfiguration()` method, as shown in the below screenshot:

Figure 7.30

Below is the screenshot showing changes required in `getProperty PaneConfiguration()` method:

```
protected getPropertyPaneConfiguration(): IPropertyPaneConfiguration {
  return {
    pages: [
      {
        header: {
          description: strings.PropertyPaneDescription
        },
        groups: [
          {
            groupName: strings.BasicGroupName,
            groupFields: [
              PropertyPaneTextField('listName', {
                label: strings.ListNameFieldLabel
              })
            ]
          }
        ]
      }
    ]
  };
}
```

Figure 7.31

10. In React-based SPFx projects, UI is served from `.tsx` file. Open `CrudReactJs. tsx` file located under `src` | `webparts` | `reactCrud` | components and make the changes for `listName` property, as shown in below screenshot:

```
export default class CrudReactJs extends React.Component<ICrudReactJsProps, {}> {
  public render(): React.ReactElement<ICrudReactJsProps> {
    return (
      <div className={ styles.crudReactJs }>
        <div className={ styles.container }>
          <div className={ styles.row }>
            <div className={ styles.column }>
              <span className={ styles.title }>Welcome to SharePoint!</span>
              <p className={ styles.subTitle }>Customize SharePoint experiences using Web Parts.</p>
              <p className={ styles.description }>{escape(this.props.listName)}</p>
              <a href="https://aka.ms/spfx" className={ styles.button }>
                <span className={ styles.label }>Learn more</span>
              </a>
            </div>
          </div>
        </div>
      </div>
    );
  }
}
```

Figure 7.32

11. In the console window (or command prompt, run the below command) to test the web part in local workbench:

```
gulp serve
```

12. Below is the screenshot showing that `listName` property is getting reflected in web part property pane:

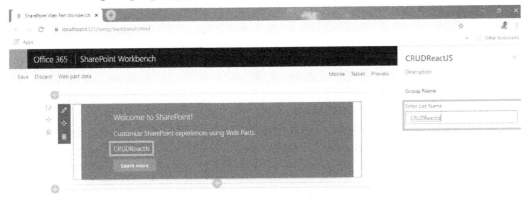

Figure 7.33

13. In this step, we will create a model for the list item. Let's add a new class (`IListItem.ts`), which will represent the list item. As shown in the below screenshot, we have added two properties of the list item, that is, `Title` and `Id`:

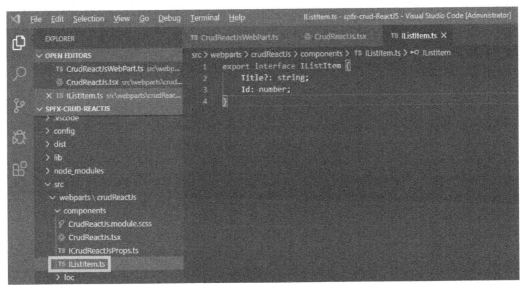

Figure 7.34

14. In this step, we will add state to our solution. Let's add a new class (`ICrudReactJsState.ts`) as shown in the following screenshot:

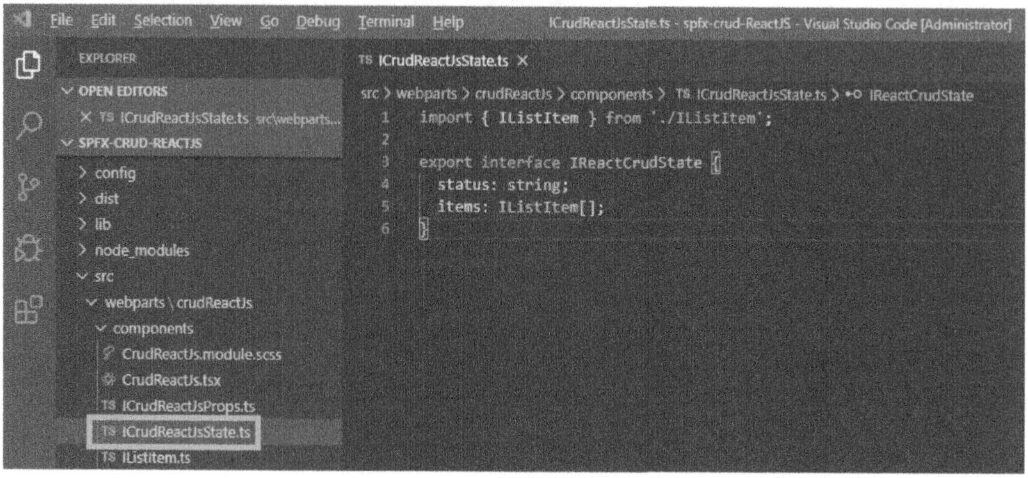

Figure 7.35

15. Add this state in `CrudReactJs.tsx` file, as shown in the below screenshot:

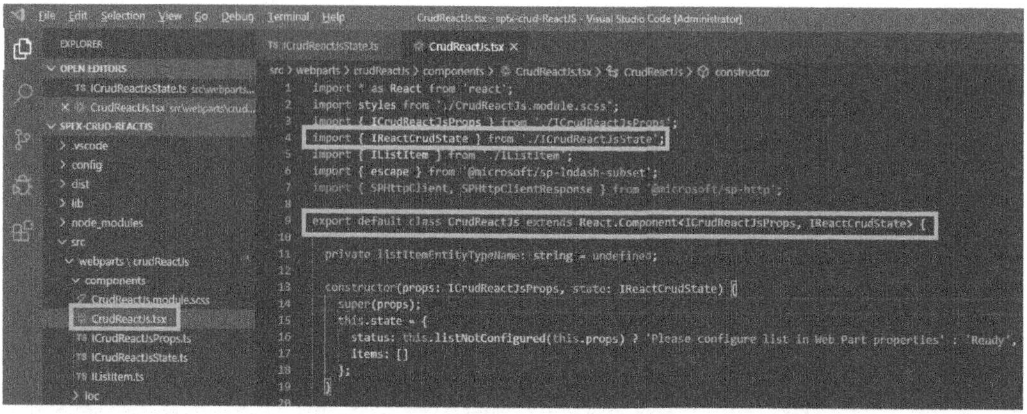

Figure 7.36

16. Modify `render()` method by adding buttons for CRUD operations and also add event handlers for each of these buttons.

Below is the image showing the modified render() method with creating, read, update, and delete buttons added along with event handlers:

```
<p className={ styles.subTitle }>using React JS.</p>
<div className={`ms-Grid-row ms-bgColor-themeDark ms-fontColor-white ${styles.row}`}>
  <div className='ms-Grid-col ms-u-lg10 ms-u-xl8 ms-u-xlPush2 ms-u-lgPush1'>
    <a href="#" className={`${styles.button}`} onClick={() => this.createItem()}>
      <span className={styles.label}>Create item</span>
    </a> 
    <a href="#" className={`${styles.button}`} onClick={() => this.readItem()}>
      <span className={styles.label}>Read item</span>
    </a>
  </div>
</div>
<div className={`ms-Grid-row ms-bgColor-themeDark ms-fontColor-white ${styles.row}`}>
  <div className='ms-Grid-col ms-u-lg10 ms-u-xl8 ms-u-xlPush2 ms-u-lgPush1'>
    <a href="#" className={`${styles.button} `} onClick={() => this.updateItem()}>
      <span className={styles.label}>Update item</span>
    </a> 
    <a href="#" className={`${styles.button} `} onClick={() => this.deleteItem()}>
      <span className={styles.label}>Delete item</span>
    </a>
  </div>
</div>
<div className={`ms-Grid-row ms-bgColor-themeDark ms-fontColor-white ${styles.row}`}>
  <div className='ms-Grid-col ms-u-lg10 ms-u-xl8 ms-u-xlPush2 ms-u-lgPush1'>
    {this.state.status}
```

Figure 7.37

17. The CRUD operations will be performed on the latest item in the SharePoint list. Update ICrudReactJsProps.ts interface IReactCrudProps.ts to include siteURL and spHttpClient, as shown in below screenshot:

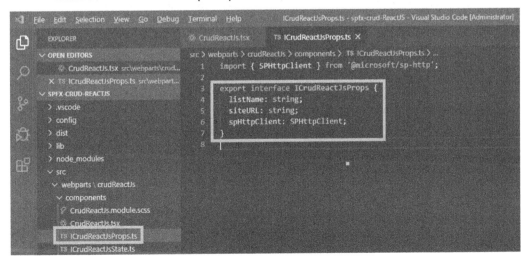

Figure 7.38

18. Update `CrudReactJsWebPart` class in `CrudReactJsWebPart.ts` file to initiate `siteURL` and `spHttpClient`, as shown in below screenshot:

```
export default class CrudReactJsWebPart extends BaseClientSideWebPart <ICrudReactJsWebPartProps> {

  public render(): void {
    const element: React.ReactElement<ICrudReactJsProps> = React.createElement(
      CrudReactJs,
      {
        listName: this.properties.listName,
        siteURL: this.context.pageContext.web.absoluteUrl,
        spHttpClient: this.context.spHttpClient
      }
    );
```

Figure 7.39

19. In this step, we will implement the `createItem()` method, which will create a new item in the SharePoint list.

    Below is the screenshot showing code of `createItem()` method in which REST API is used to create a new item in the SharePoint list:

```
private createItem(): void {
  this.setState({
    status1: 'Creating item...',
    items: []
  });

  this.getListItemEntityTypeName()
    .then((listItemEntityTypeName: string): Promise<SPHttpClientResponse> => {
      const body: string = JSON.stringify({
        '__metadata': {
          'type': listItemEntityTypeName
        },
        'Title': `Item ${new Date()}`
      });
      return this.props.spHttpClient.post(`${this.props.siteURL}/_api/web/lists/getbytitle('${this.props.listName}')/items`,
        SPHttpClient.configurations.v1,
        {
          headers: {
            'Accept': 'application/json;odata=nometadata',
            'Content-type': 'application/json;odata=verbose',
            'odata-version': ''
          },
          body: body
        });
    })
    .then((response: SPHttpClientResponse): Promise<IListItem> => {
      return response.json();
    })
    .then((item: IListItem): void => {
      this.setState({
        status1: `Item '${item.Title}' (ID: ${item.Id}) successfully created`,
        items: []
```

Figure 7.40

20. In this step, we will implement the `readItem()` method, which will read the latest item from a SharePoint list.

Below is the screenshot showing code of readItem() method in which REST API is used to read the latest item from SharePoint list:

```
private readItem(): void {
  this.setState({
    status1: 'Loading latest items...',
    items: []
  });
  this.getLatestItemId()
    .then((itemId: number): Promise<SPHttpClientResponse> => {
      if (itemId === -1) {
        throw new Error('No items found in the list');
      }

      this.setState({
        status1: `Loading information about item ID: ${itemId}...`,
        items: []
      });
      return this.props.spHttpClient.get(`${this.props.siteURL}/_api/web/lists/getbytitle('${this.props.listName}')/items(${itemId})?$select+Ti
        SPHttpClient.configurations.v1,
        {
          headers: {
            'Accept': 'application/json;odata=nometadata',
            'odata-version': ''
          }
        });
    })
    .then((response: SPHttpClientResponse): Promise<IListItem> => {
      return response.json();
    })
    .then((item: IListItem): void => {
      this.setState({
        status1: `Item ID: ${item.Id}, Title: ${item.Title}`,
        items: []
```

Figure 7.41

21. In this step, we will implement the updateItem() method, which will update the latest item from a SharePoint list.

Below is the screenshot showing code of updateItem() method to update the latest item:

```
private updateItem(): void {
  this.setState({
    status1: 'Loading latest items...',
    items: []
  });
  let latestItemId: number = undefined;
  let etag: string = undefined;
  let listItemEntityTypeName: string = undefined;
  this.getListItemEntityTypeName()
    .then((listItemType: string): Promise<number> => {
      listItemEntityTypeName = listItemType;
      return this.getLatestItemId();
    })
    .then((itemId: number): Promise<SPHttpClientResponse> => {
      if (itemId === -1) {
        throw new Error('No items found in the list');
      }

      latestItemId = itemId;
      this.setState({
        status1: `Loading information about item ID: ${latestItemId}...`,
        items: []
      });
      return this.props.spHttpClient.get(`${this.props.siteURL}/_api/web/lists/getbytitle('${this.props.listName}')/items(${latestItemId})?$sele
        SPHttpClient.configurations.v1,
        {
          headers: {
            'Accept': 'application/json;odata=nometadata',
            'odata-version': ''
          }
        });
```

Figure 7.42

22. In this step, we will implement the `deleteItem()` method, which will delete the latest item from a SharePoint list.

    Below is the screenshot showing code of `deleteItem()` method in which REST API is used to delete the latest item from SharePoint list:

```
private deleteItem(): void {
  if (!window.confirm('Are you sure you want to delete the latest item?')) {
    return;
  }

  this.setState({
    status1: 'Loading latest items...',
    items: []
  });
  let latestItemId: number = undefined;
  let etag: string = undefined;
  this.getLatestItemId()
    .then((itemId: number): Promise<SPHttpClientResponse> => {
      if (itemId === -1) {
        throw new Error('No items found in the list');
      }

      latestItemId = itemId;
      this.setState({
        status1: `Loading information about item ID: ${latestItemId}...`,
        items: []
      });
      return this.props.spHttpClient.get(`${this.props.siteURL}/_api/web/lists/getbytitle('${this.props.listName}')/items(${latestItemId})?$sele
        SPHttpClient.configurations.v1,
        {
          headers: {
            'Accept': 'application/json;odata=nometadata',
            'odata-version': ''
          }
        });
    })
    .then((response: SPHttpClientResponse): Promise<IListItem> => {
```

Figure 7.43

23. In the command prompt, type the command `gulp serve` to test the SPFx web part on SharePoint workbench (`<your-site-url>/_layouts/workbench.aspx`). Click on the buttons (**Create item, Read item, Update item, and Delete item**) to test the webpart and verify that the respective operations are taking place in a SharePoint list.

    Below is the screenshot showing **Create item** operation in the web part:

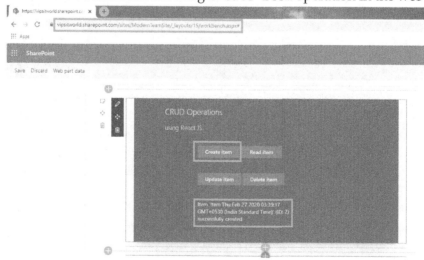

Figure 7.44

Below is the screenshot showing an item is created in a SharePoint list:

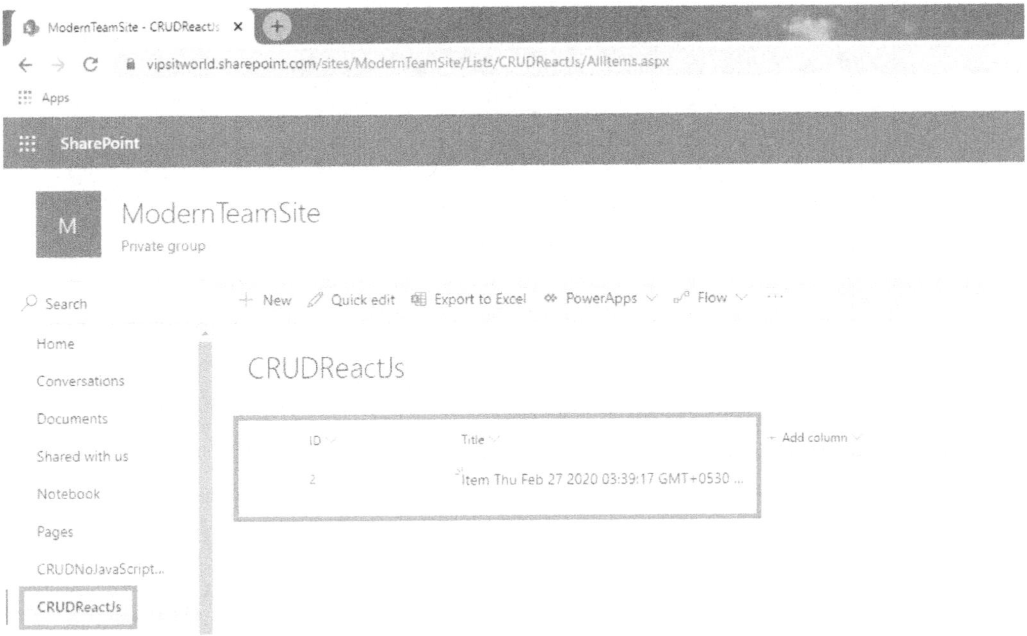

Figure 7.45

Below is the screenshot showing **Read item** operation in the web part:

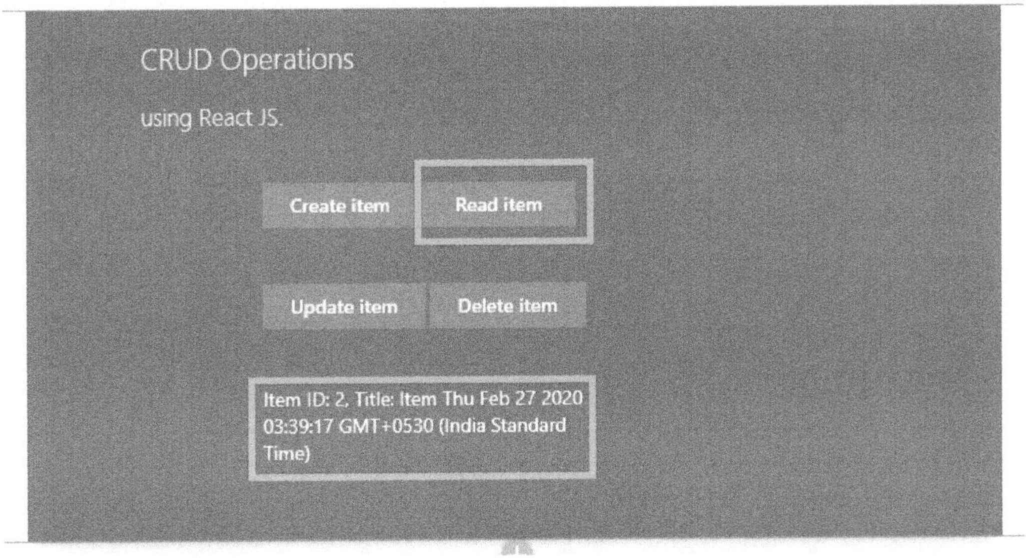

Figure 7.46

Below is the image showing **Update item** operation in the web part:

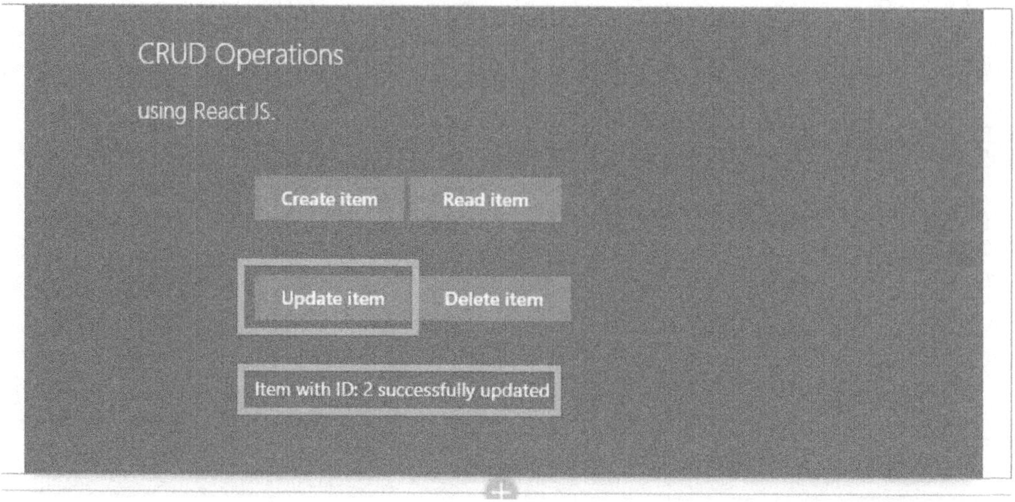

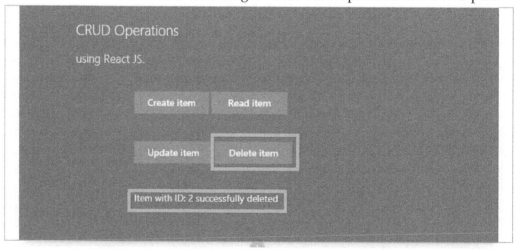

Figure 7.47

Below is the screenshot showing **Delete item** operation in the web part:

Figure 7.48

Conclusion

In this chapter, we discussed how to implement CRUD (Create, Read, Update, Delete) operations using No JavaScript Framework. REST APIs can be used to perform the CRUD operations on a SharePoint list. We also understood the core concepts of React JS required for development in the SharePoint Framework client-side web parts. Finally, we discussed implementing CRUD operations using React JS as JavaScript Framework. In the next chapter, we will discuss Logging and Debugging in SPFx web parts.

Points to remember

- Use the MERGE value in the X-HTTP-Method property while implementing Update operation.
- You can implement CRUD operations with No JavaScript Framework, React JS, Angular JS, Knockout JS, and so on.
- Use the SharePoint context SPHttpClient to call SharePoint REST APIs.
- Use ETags to ensure data integrity when updating and deleting items.

Multiple Choice Questions

1. What is the declarative way to render a dynamic list of components based on values in an array?
    - *a.* Using the reduce array method
    - *b.* With a for/while loop
    - *c.* Using the <Each /> component
    - *d.* Using the Array.map() method
2. Which of the below act as the input of a class-based component?
    - *a.* class and factory
    - *b.* render and mount
    - *c.* props
    - *d.* None of these

Answer

1. D
2. C

Questions

1. What are the advantages of using React JS?
2. What are props and state in React JS?
3. How is the React-based SPFx solution structure different from No JavaScript Framework SPFx solution structure?

Key terms

- **CRUD:** Create, Read, Update, and Delete.

CHAPTER 8

Logging and Debugging in SPFx Web Parts

Everything looks fine till the time your web part works as expected; however, it becomes tedious to identify errors when any of the user requests fails, and the web part starts displaying error messages or exceptions. Hence, developers should implement logging while writing code in their projects, which allows them to keep track of events happening in the web part.

SharePoint supports logging by default, and similarly, SharePoint Framework includes a built-in logging mechanism. On the other hand, debugging allows you to traverse through your code using breakpoints and allows you to fix errors efficiently.

In this chapter, we will discuss implementing logging and debugging in the SharePoint Framework web parts.

Structure

In this chapter, we will cover the following topics:

- SharePoint Framework logging mechanism
- Debugging SPFx web parts using Visual Studio Code

Objective

After studying this chapter, you should be able to:

- Implement lLogging in your SPFx solution
- Debug SPFx web parts in Visual Studio Code

SharePoint Framework lLogging mechanism

In SharePoint Framework, all logging is done to the JavaScript console, and you can see the logging using the developer tools (*F12* in Google Chrome browser) in a web browser.

The `Log` class contains four static methods for logging, as shown in the below table:

Method name	Description
Info	This method logs information to monitor the state of the solution.
Warn	This method logs warnings, which highlights potential issues.
Error	This method logs errors and highlights significant issues.
Verbose	This method logs everything.

Table 8.1

All the above methods have the same signature; that is, they take three arguments.

Below table shows the type of arguments taken by the Log class methods:

Source	The source of the logging information (max 20 characters), such as the method or the class name
Message	The actual message to log (max 100 characters)
Scope	An optional service scope

Table 8.2

The error method takes an Error object instead of the message string.

Below are the steps to create an SPFx web part solution for implementing logging.

1. Create a directory for SPFx solution using the below command:

   ```
   md spfx-Logging
   ```

2. Navigate to the directory created in *Step 1* using the below command:

   ```
   cd spfx-Logging
   ```

3. Use the below command to run Yeoman SharePoint Generator to create the solution:

```
yo @microsoft/sharepoint
```

4. Provide below values in the Yeoman generator wizard:

   - **Solution Name:** Select default value by pressing *Enter*
   - **The target for the component:** SharePoint Online only (latest)
   - **Place of files:** Current folder
   - **Deployment option:** *N* to install on each site explicitly
   - **Permission to access Web APIs:** *N* to avoid granting permissions to access Web APIs
   - **Type of client-side component to create:** WebPart
   - **Web part name:** SPFxLogging
   - **Web part description:** Select default value by pressing *Enter*
   - **The framework to use:** No JavaScript Framework

5. Once the Yeoman generator finishes generating the solution, open the solution in Visual Studio Code editor using `code .` command.

6. Add the below import statement in main web part file (`SpFxLoggingWebPart.ts`) to import the `Log` class:

```
import { Log } from '@microsoft/sp-core-library';
```

7. Define the log source and method, as shown in the following screenshot:

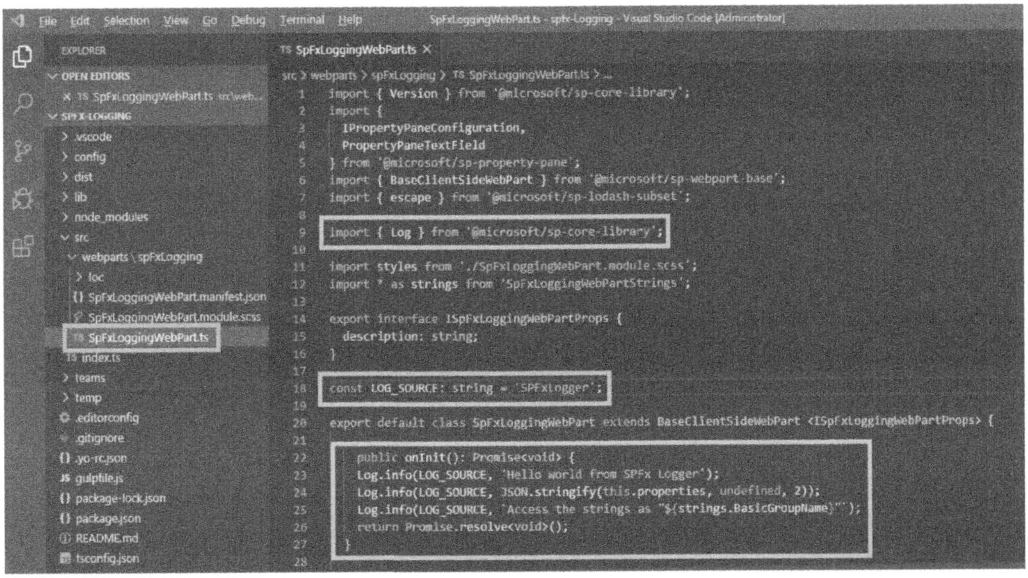

Figure 8.1

8. Run `gulp serve` in command prompt and add the web part on the local workbench. Open developer tools and check that logs are added and shown in the browser console window.

Below is the screenshot showing custom logs which are added in SPFx web part:

Figure 8.2

Debugging SPFx web parts using Visual Studio Code

The best way to debug your code in Visual Studio code editor is by using the Visual Studio Code extension called **Debugger for Chrome**. With the latest versions of SPFx, this extension gets installed by default in Visual Studio Code.

To verify, open your SPFx solution in Visual Studio Code editor and click on **Extension** on the left menu. Search for **Debugger for Chrome** extension and install it, if not already.

Below is the screenshot showing the debug extension in Visual Studio Code:

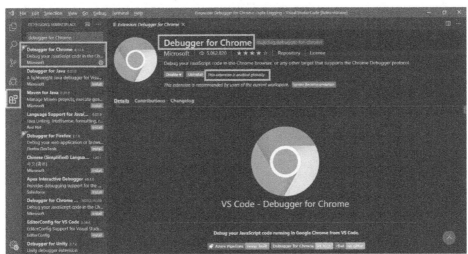

Figure 8.3

You need to have the above extension installed to start debugging in the Visual Studio Code. You can also install Debugger for Edge Visual Studio extension if you are debugging in the Edge browser.

The required debug configurations are included in SPFx solutions by default. These debug configurations are available in the `.vscode` folder in the `launch.json` file present in your SPFx solution.

Below is the screenshot showing `launch.json` file in SPFx solution:

Figure 8.4

As you can see in *Figure 8.4*, there are two different configurations available for debugging in the `launch.json` file. There is a separate configuration for `Local workbench`, which is pointing to the localhost URL. Then there is another debug configuration for Hosted workbench, which is pointing to your SharePoint site workbench URL.

Follow the below steps to debug in Local workbench:

1. Go to main web part file (`SpFxLoggingWebPart.ts`) in `src` folder and put a breakpoint at one the line, as shown in the following screenshot (breakpoint is highlighted in the green box):

Figure 8.5

2. Open the terminal (Go to **View > Terminal** OR directly click **Terminal** menu of Visual Studio Code) in Visual Studio Code.

    Below is the screenshot showing how to open **Terminal** in Visual Studio Code editor:

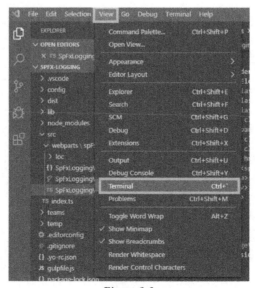

Figure 8.6

3. Run the solution using the below command:

```
gulp serve --nobrowser
```

Below is the screenshot showing Terminal with the above command:

Figure 8.7

4. Now since `gulp serve` is running, we can start debugging the solution. For this, go to debug tab on the left menu (you can also start debugging by hitting *F5* from the keyboard or **Debug** menu of Visual Studio Code) and press **RUN AND DEBUG**, as shown in below screenshot:

Figure 8.8

5. The moment you will start debugging, a browser window will open and local workbench will show up and will allow you to add the web part, as shown in below screenshot:

Figure 8.9

6. Notice in below image that breakpoint color has been changed because local workbench is popped up and till now, we have not added the web part on the local workbench:

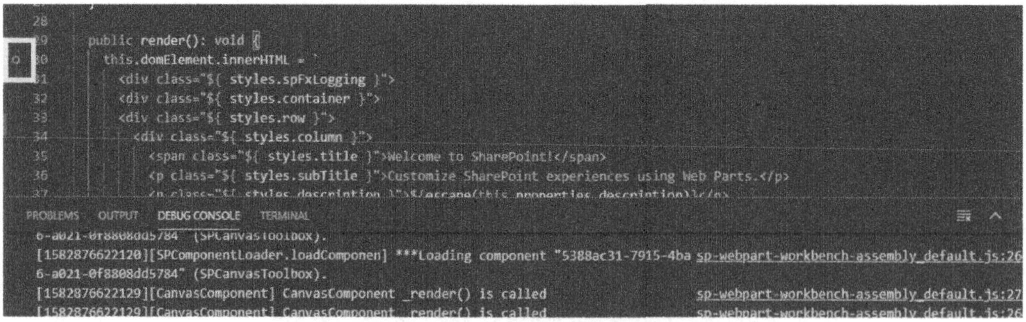

Figure 8.10

7. Add the web part and notice that breakpoint color again turns to red and debugging starts in Visual Studio Code, as shown in the following screenshot:

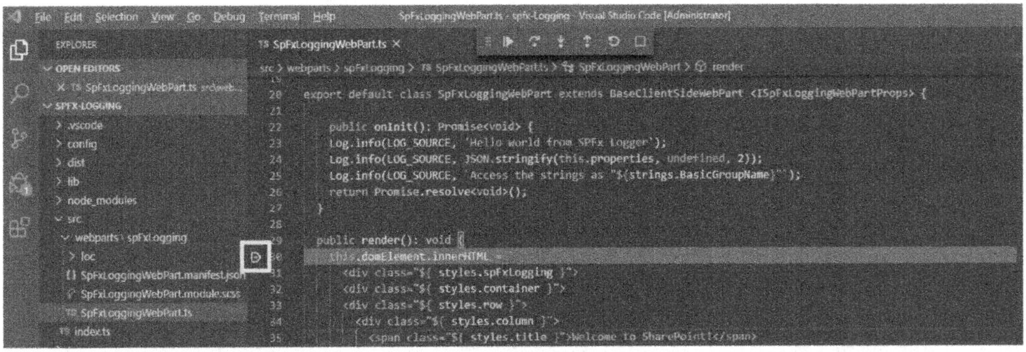

Figure 8.11

Also, below screenshot shows that screen is paused in local workbench as debugging is in progress:

Figure 8.12

In Visual Studio, while debugging, you can check the different properties of this as shown in the following screenshot:

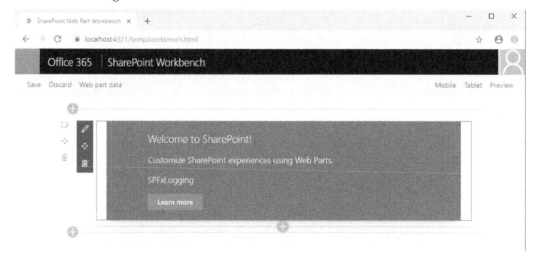

Figure 8.13

8. Once you press F5, the web part will be added on the page, as shown in the following screenshot:

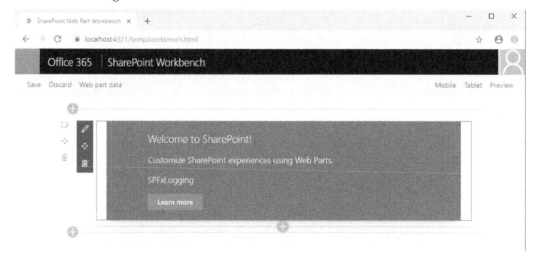

Figure 8.14

Every time you click on the web part for modifications, or on edit web part button (in the reactive web part, render() methods get called again), the breakpoint will be hit.

9. Stop the debugging session by clicking on **Stop Debugging** in the **Debug** menu of the Visual Studio Code.

Follow the below steps to debug in Hosted workbench:

1. All other steps remain the same as of local workbench, except that in launch. json file, you need to specify the URL of your SharePoint Hosted workbench, as shown in below screenshot:

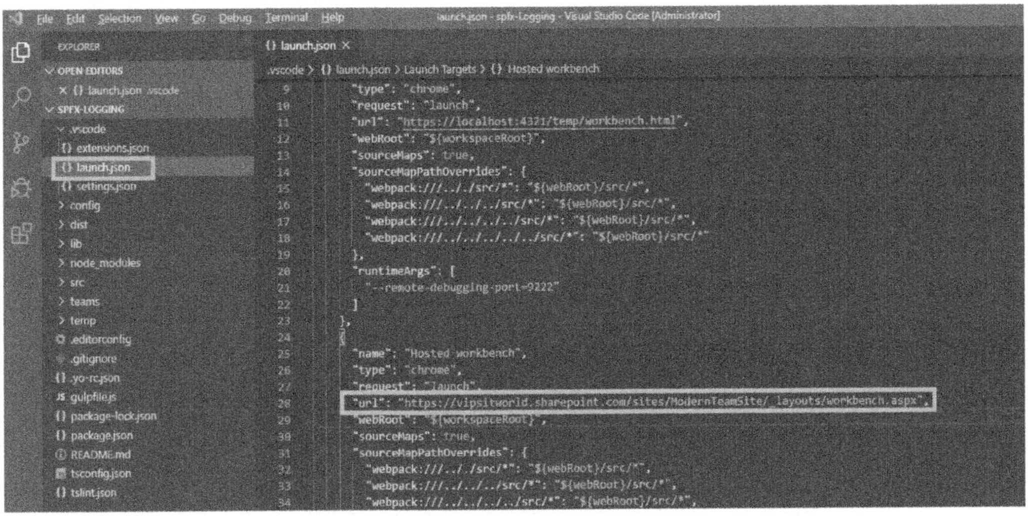

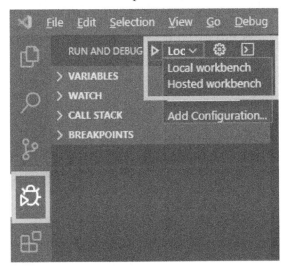

Figure 8.15

2. Second change required is that in **Debug** menu on the left, you need to select **Hosted workbench** from the drop-down, as shown in the below screenshot:

Figure 8.16

In the Hosted workbench, once browser session starts, then you need to sign with credentials (as the browser will open in Incognito mode) because of -incognito" property present in hosted workbench configuration in `launch.json` file

Conclusion

In this chapter, we discussed the logging and debugging mechanism for the SPFx web part. We discussed that SharePoint Framework provides out-of-the-box API to log information in your SPFx solutions. In the next chapter, we will see some examples of SharePoint Framework web parts.

Points to remember

- SharePoint Framework provides out-of-the-box API to log information in your SPFx solutions.
- You can debug SPFx solutions both in local and hosted workbench.

Multiple Choice Questions

1. Which Log class method logs everything in SharePoint Framework?
   a. info
   b. warn
   c. verbose
   d. error

2. Which file contains debug configurations in an SPFx web part solution?
   a. launch.json
   b. serve.json
   c. config.json
   d. write-manifests.json

Answer

1. C
2. A

Questions

1. What are the different methods that the Log class provides, and what are their uses?

Key terms

- **Hosted workbench:** In the hosted workbench, you can preview and test your SPFx web part by interacting with SharePoint objects.

CHAPTER 9

SharePoint Framework Web Part Examples

In this chapter, we will explore different SPFx web part examples and will see how we can integrate jQuery in SPFx web parts and can build the Microsoft Teams tab using SharePoint Framework.

Structure

In this chapter, we will cover the following topics:

- Implementing jQueryUI accordion
- Building Microsoft Teams tab using SharePoint Framework

Objective

After studying this chapter, you should be able to:

- Integrate jQuery in SPFx web part
- Implement Microsoft Teams Tab in SPFx web part

Implementing jQueryUI accordion

Follow below steps to integrate jQuery in SPFx web part:

1. Create a directory for SPFx solution using the following command:

```
md jquery-accordion
```

2. Navigate to the directory created in *Step 1* using the following command:

`cd jquery- accordion`

3. Use the following command to run the Yeoman SharePoint Generator to create the solution:

`yo @microsoft/sharepoint`

4. Provide below values in the Yeoman generator wizard
   - **Solution Name:** Select default value by pressing *Enter*
   - **The target for the component:** SharePoint Online only (latest)
   - **Place of files:** Current folder
   - **Deployment option:** *N* to install on each site explicitly
   - **Permission to access Web APIs:** *N* to avoid granting permissions to access Web APIs
   - **Type of client-side component to create:** WebPart
   - **Web part name:** SPFxJqueryAccordion
   - **Web part description:** Select default value by pressing *Enter*
   - **The framework to use:** No JavaScript Framework

5. Once the Yeoman generator finishes generating the solution, open the solution in Visual Studio Code editor using `code .` command.

6. In the console window, enter the following command to install the jQuery and jQueryUI NPM packages:

`npm install jquery@2 jqueryui --save`

7. In the console window, enter the below command to install the required typings:

`npm install @types/jquery@2`

8. The following screenshot shows that NPM packages for jQuery and jQueryUI are added in the `node_modules` folder:

> This PC › New Volume (D:) › Vipul › demos › jquery-accordion › node_modules ›

Name	Date modified	Type	Size
jest-validate	29-02-2020 00:42	File folder	
jest-watcher	29-02-2020 00:41	File folder	
jest-worker	29-02-2020 00:41	File folder	
jju	29-02-2020 00:42	File folder	
jquery	29-02-2020 00:48	File folder	
jqueryui	29-02-2020 00:48	File folder	
js-base64	29-02-2020 00:42	File folder	

Figure 9.1

9. In Visual Studio Code, open the file config | config.json. In externals section, add the jQuery references, as shown in the following screenshot:

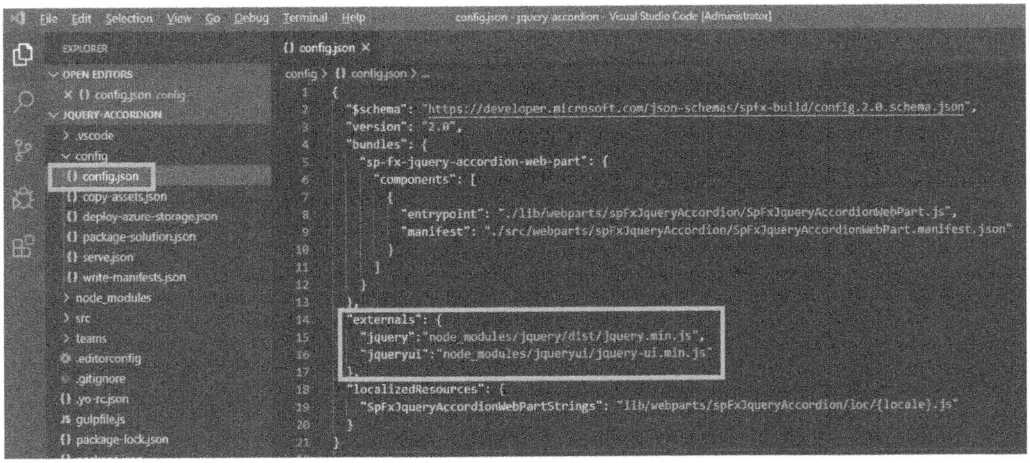

Figure 9.2

10. Add a new file in the src | webparts | spFxJqueryAccordion folder called AccordionCode.ts

11. Create a class AccordionCode that holds the HTML code for the jQuery accordion, as shown in the following screenshot and save the file:

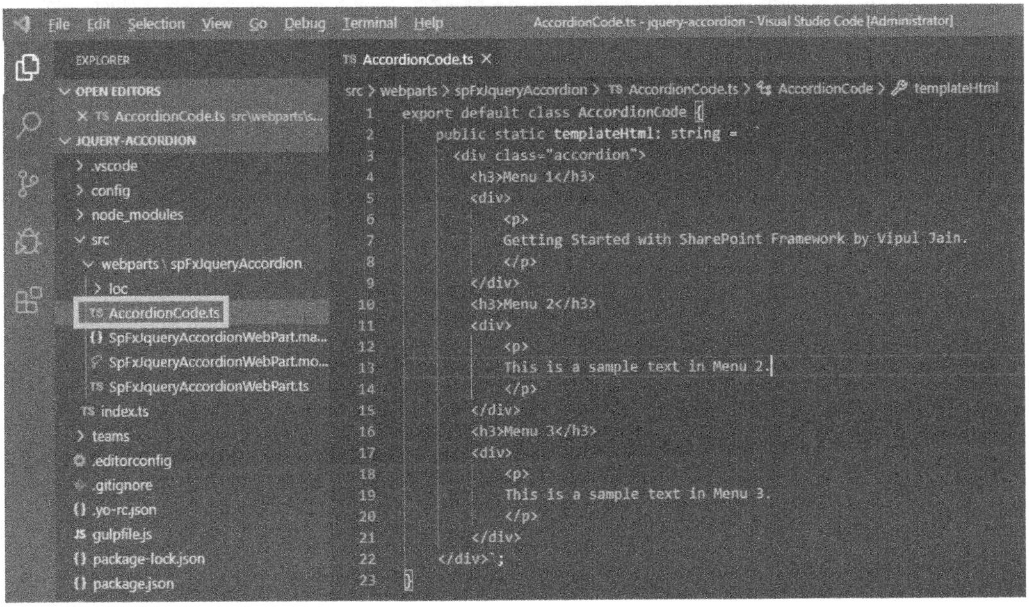

Figure 9.3

12. Open src | webparts | spFxJqueryAccordion | SpFxJqueryAccordion WebPart.ts and import the AccordionCode class added in the previous step.

13. Import jQuery and jqueryui in the main web part file, as shown in the following screenshot:

```
import AccordionCode from './AccordionCode';

import * as jQuery from 'jquery';
import 'jqueryui';
```

Figure 9.4

14. Add the following import statement to load some external CSS:

```
import { SPComponentLoader } from '@microsoft/sp-loader';
```

15. Add a constructor and load external jQuery UI CSS from it, as shown in the below screenshot:

```
export default class SpFxJqueryAccordionWebPart extends BaseClientSideWebPart <ISpFxJqueryAccordionWebPartProps> {

  public constructor() {
    super();

    SPComponentLoader.loadCss('//code.jquery.com/ui/1.11.4/themes/smoothness/jquery-ui.css');
  }
```

Figure 9.5

16. Comment the existing code in `render()` method and add the code, as shown in the below screenshot:

```
public render(): void {

    this.domElement.innerHTML = AccordionCode.templateHtml;

    const accordionOptions: JQueryUI.AccordionOptions = {
      animate: true,
      collapsible: false,
      icons: {
        header: 'ui-icon-circle-arrow-e',
        activeHeader: 'ui-icon-circle-arrow-s'
      }
    };

    jQuery('.accordion', this.domElement).accordion(accordionOptions);

    /*
    this.domElement.innerHTML = `
      <div class="${ styles.spFxJQueryAccordion }">
      <div class="${ styles.container }">
        <div class="${ styles.row }">
          <div class="${ styles.column }">
            <span class="${ styles.title }">Welcome to SharePoint!</span>
            <p class="${ styles.subTitle }">Customize SharePoint experiences using Web Parts.</p>
            <p class="${ styles.description }">${escape(this.properties.description)}</p>
            <a href="https://aka.ms/spfx" class="${ styles.button }">
              <span class="${ styles.label }">Learn more</span>
            </a>
          </div>
        </div>
      </div>
    </div>`;*/
}
```

Figure 9.6

17. On the command prompt, type `gulp serve` and test the web part on the local workbench.

The following screenshot shows that jQuery accordion web part is added on the local workbench:

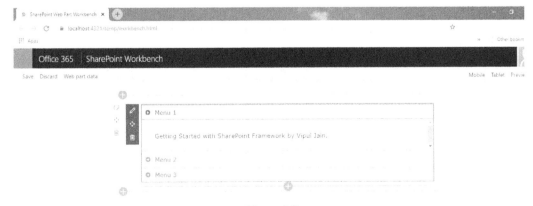

Figure 9.7

Building Microsoft Teams tab using SharePoint Framework

With the release of SharePoint Framework, v1.8, you can build Microsoft Teams tabs using SharePoint Framework.

Follow below steps to build Microsoft Teams tab using SharePoint Framework:

1. Create a directory for SPFx solution using the below command:

    ```
    md spfx-msteams-tab
    ```

2. Navigate to the directory created in *Step 1* using the below command:

    ```
    cd spfx-msteams-tab
    ```

3. Use the below command to run Yeoman SharePoint Generator to create the solution:

    ```
    yo @microsoft/sharepoint
    ```

4. Provide below values in the Yeoman generator wizard:

    *   **Solution Name:** Select default value by pressing Enter
    *   **The target for the component:** SharePoint Online only (latest)
    *   **Place of files:** Current folder
    *   **Deployment option:** *Y* to deploy on each site instantly and will be accessible everywhere
    *   **Permission to access Web APIs:** *N* to avoid granting permissions to access Web APIs
    *   **Type of client-side component to create:** WebPart
    *   **Web part name:** SPFxTeamsTab
    *   **Web part description:** Select default value by pressing *Enter*
    *   **The framework to use:** No JavaScript Framework

5. Once the Yeoman generator finishes generating the solution, open the solution in Visual Studio Code editor using `code` . command.

6. Open web part `manifest.json` file. In the "`supportedHosts`" property, add "`TeamsTab`", as shown in the following screenshot:

Figure 9.8

7. Open the web part file (`src` | `webparts` | `spFxTeamsTab` | `SpFxTeamsTabWebPart.ts`) and below import statement:

```
import * as microsoftTeams from '@microsoft/teams-js';
```

8. Define a variable to store Microsoft Teams context, as shown below:

```
private _context: microsoftTeams.Context;
```

9. Modify the `render` method, as shown in the following screenshot:

```
public render(): void {
    let webPartTitle: string = '';
    let siteTitle: string = '';

    if (this._context) {
        // Teams Context
        webPartTitle = "Welcome to Teams!";
        siteTitle = "Teams Name: " + this._context.teamName;
    }
    else
    {
        // SharePoint Context
        webPartTitle = "Welcome to SharePoint!";
        siteTitle = "SharePoint site: " + this.context.pageContext.web.title;
    }

    this.domElement.innerHTML = `
        <div class="${ styles.spFxTeamsTab }">
            <div class="${ styles.container }">
                <div class="${ styles.row }">
                    <div class="${ styles.column }">
                        <span class="${ styles.title }">${webPartTitle}</span>
                        <p class="${ styles.subTitle }">${siteTitle}</p>
                        <p class="${ styles.description }">${escape(this.properties.description)}</p>
                        <a href="https://aka.ms/spfx" class="${ styles.button }">
                            <span class="${ styles.label }">Learn more</span>
                        </a>
                    </div>
                </div>
            </div>
        </div>`;
}
```

Figure 9.9

The same web part can work in SharePoint and Microsoft Teams context.

10. In the command prompt, run the below command to bundle the solution:

```
gulp bundle --ship
```

11. In the command prompt, run the below command to package the solution:

```
gulp package-solution --ship
```

12. Open the SharePoint app catalog site and upload the .sppkg to the app catalog. Check "**Make this solution available to all sites in the organization**" option, as shown in the following screenshot:

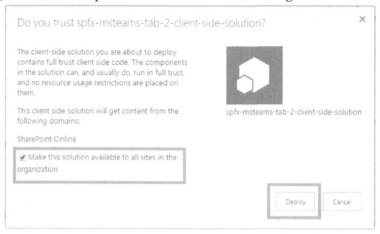

Figure 9.10

13. Click **Deploy**.

14. Add the web part to the SharePoint site. The following screenshot shows that teams web parts get added on a SharePoint page:

Figure 9.11

15. To make the web part available in Microsoft Teams, the SPFx solution needs to be synchronized with teams. Select the solution in the app catalog and from the ribbon, in the **FILES** tab, select "" option, as shown in the following screenshot:

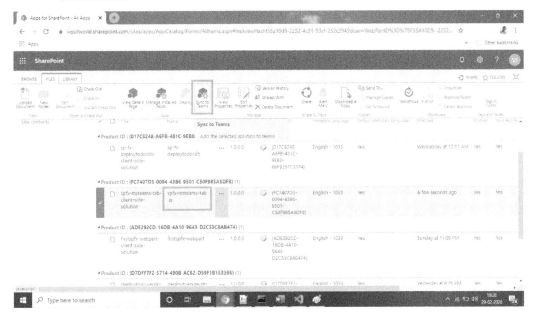

Figure 9.12

16. Open Microsoft Teams. Create a new Team or use the existing one. Inside this team, select a channel (by default, **General** channel is available under team) and then click on + to add a new tab, as shown in the following screenshot:

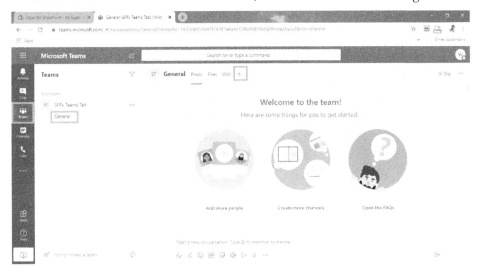

Figure 9.13

17. Select your custom teams tab from the available list, as shown in the following screenshot:

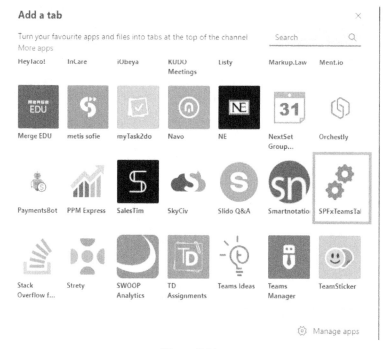

Figure 9.14

18. Click on **Add**, as shown in the following screenshot:

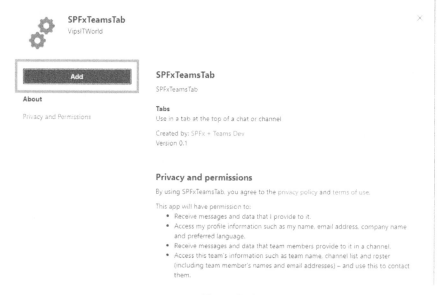

Figure 9.15

19. Click on **Save** to save your teams tab, as shown in the following screenshot:

Figure 9.16

20. Your web part will start appearing as a custom tab in Microsoft Teams, as shown in the following screenshot:

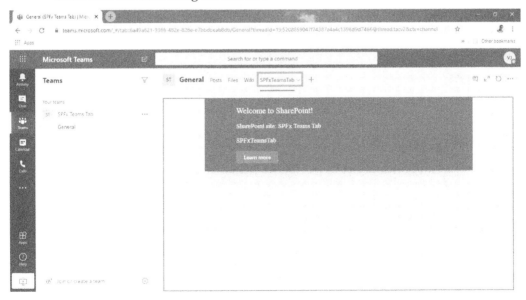

Figure 9.17

Conclusion

In this chapter, we discussed a couple of examples of SPFx web parts, including integrating jQuery and jQueryUI in the SharePoint Framework and implementing the Microsoft Teams tab using SPFx and how you can use Teams web part both in SharePoint and Microsoft Teams context. JavaScript frameworks support typings, which helps developers in IntelliSense while writing the code in editors. In the next chapter, we will discuss SharePoint Framework extensions and its different types.

Points to remember

- Refer to external libraries like jQuery and jQueryUI in the `Externals` section in the `config.json` file. It will not include these libraries in the final bundle of the web part.

- While scaffolding SPFx solution (using Yeoman), but the answer as Y in the `Deployment` option while working with Microsoft Teams tab.

Multiple Choice Questions

1. In which file you specify "`supportedHosts`" property as "`TeamsTab`"?

    a. config.json

    b. Web part manifest.json

    c. launch.json

    d. package-solution.json

Answer

1. B

Questions

1. How can you connect to Microsoft Teams in the SharePoint Framework web part?

Key terms

- **jQuery, jQueryUI:** These are the JavaScript frameworks that integrate very well with SharePoint Framework web parts.

CHAPTER 10

Overview of SharePoint Framework Extensions

SharePoint Framework Extensions allow developers to extend or enhance the SharePoint user experience (in terms of look and feel). You can customize SharePoint user experience involving the notification area, list views, and toolbars. In this chapter, we will see how to use Application Customizers, Field Customizers, and Command Sets.

Structure

In this chapter, we will cover the following topics:

- Overview of SharePoint Framework Extensions
- Develop your first Application Customizer
- Develop your first Field Customizer
- Develop a ListView Command Set extension

Objective

After studying this chapter, you should be able to:

- Implement different types of SharePoint Framework extensions
- Customize SharePoint UI as per the modern standards

Overview of SharePoint Framework Extensions

SharePoint Framework includes three extension types:

1. Application Customizers
   - It allows inserting custom HTML to well-known locations (header and footer) on the page (HTML element placeholders)
   - It allows injecting custom scripts on the page

2. Field Customizers
   - It allows modifying views to data for fields within a list

3. Command sets
   - It allows inserting custom commands to Lists' command bar (toolbar)
   - It allows inserting custom commands to List Items' context menu (ECB)

To update your SharePoint Framework Yeoman generator, you the below command:

```
npm update -g @microsoft/generator-sharepoint@latest
```

Develop your first application customizer

Follow the below steps to develop your first Application customizer:

1. Create a directory for SPFx solution using the below command:
   ```
   md spfx-applicationcustomizer
   ```

2. Navigate to the directory created in Step-1 using the below command:
   ```
   cd spfx-applicationcustomizer
   ```

3. Use the below command to run Yeoman SharePoint Generator to create the solution:
   ```
   yo @microsoft/sharepoint
   ```

4. Provide below values in the Yeoman generator wizard
   - **Solution Name:** Select default value by pressing *Enter*
   - **The target for the component:** SharePoint Online only (latest)
   - **Place of files:** Current folder
   - **Deployment option:** *N* to install on each site explicitly
   - **Permission to access Web APIs:** *N* to avoid granting permissions to access Web APIs

- **Type of client-side component to create:** Extension

- **Type of client-side extension to create:** Application Customizer

- **Application Customizer name:** HelloWorld

- **Application Customizer description:** Select default value by pressing *Enter*

5. Once the Yeoman generator finishes generating the solution, open the solution in Visual Studio Code editor using `code .` command.

6. Open the `HelloWorldApplicationCustomizer.manifest.json` in the `src\extensions\helloWorld` folder. This file contains information about `componentType`, `extensionType`, `alias`, and `id`, as shown in the following screenshot:

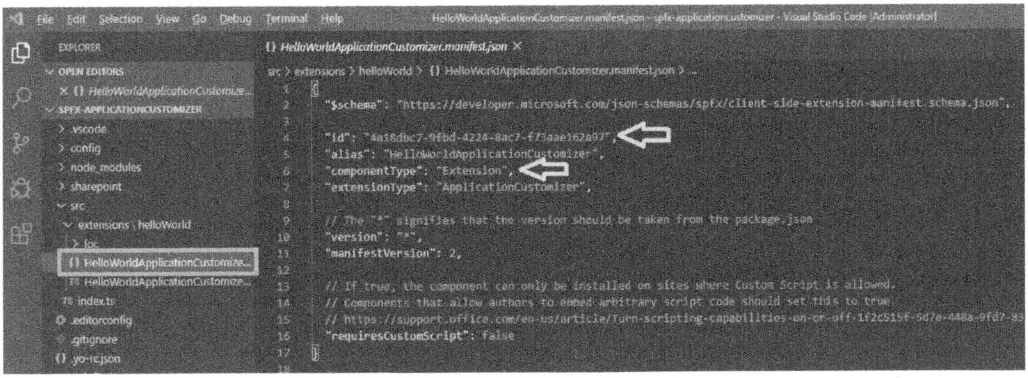

Figure 10.1

7. Open `HelloWorldApplicationCustomizer.ts` file located under `\src\extensions\helloWorld` and add the import statements (required to get access to page placeholders), as shown in the following screenshot:

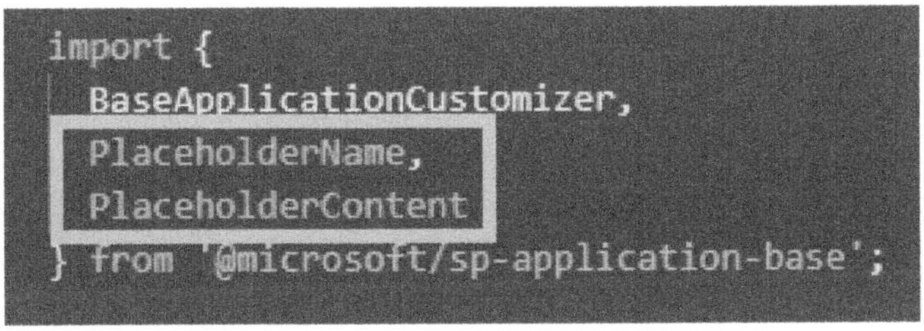

Figure 10.2

8. Update the interface `IHelloWorldApplicationCustomizerProperties` to include `Top` and `Bottom` properties, as shown in the following screenshot:

```
export interface IHelloWorldApplicationCustomizerProperties {
  // This is an example; replace with your own property
  //testMessage: string;
  Top: string;
  Bottom: string;
}
```

Figure 10.3

9. Update the code of `onInit()` method, as shown in the following screenshot:

```
@override
public onInit(): Promise<void> {
  Log.info(LOG_SOURCE, `Initialized ${strings.Title}`);

  this.context.placeholderProvider.changedEvent.add(this, this._renderPlaceHolders);

  return Promise.resolve<void>();
}
```

Figure 10.4

10. Add the following code in `_renderPlaceHolders` method:

```
private _renderPlaceHolders(): void{
    console.log("HelloWorldApplicationCustomizer._
renderPlaceHolders()");
    console.log(
      "Available placeholders: ",
      this.context.placeholderProvider.placeholderNames
        .map(name => PlaceholderName[name])
        .join(", ")
    );


    // Handling the top placeholder
    if (!this._topPlaceholder) {
      this._topPlaceholder = this.context.placeholderProvider.
tryCreateContent(
```

```
            PlaceholderName.Top,
            { onDispose: this._onDispose }
        );


        // The extension should not assume that the expected
placeholder is available.
        if (!this._topPlaceholder) {
            console.error("The expected placeholder (Top) was not
found.");
            return;
        }


        if (this.properties) {
            let customtopString : string = this.properties.Top;
            if (!customtopString) {
                customtopString = "(Top property was not defined.)";
            }


            if (this._topPlaceholder.domElement) {
                this._topPlaceholder.domElement.innerHTML = `
                <div class="${styles.app}">
                    <div class="${styles.top}">
                        <i class="ms-Icon ms-Icon--Info" aria-
hidden="true"></i> ${escape(
                            customtopString
                        )}
                    </div>
                </div>`;
            }
        }


        // Handling the bottom placeholder
        if (!this._bottomPlaceholder) {
```

```
      this._bottomPlaceholder = this.context.
placeholderProvider.tryCreateContent(

      PlaceholderName.Bottom,

      { onDispose: this._onDispose }

      );


      // The extension should not assume that the expected
placeholder is available.
      if (!this._bottomPlaceholder) {

      console.error("The expected placeholder (Bottom) was
not found.");

      return;

      }


      if (this.properties) {
       let custombottomString : string = this.properties.Bottom;
        if (!custombottomString) {
        custombottomString = "(Bottom property was not defined.)";

        }


      if (this._bottomPlaceholder.domElement) {
         this._bottomPlaceholder.domElement.innerHTML = `
        <div class="${styles.app}">
          <div class="${styles.bottom}">
            <i class="ms-Icon ms-Icon--Info" aria-
hidden="true"></i> ${escape(
              custombottomString
            )}
          </div>
          </div>`;
      }
      }
    }
    }
```

Following are some of the important points about this code:

- `this.context.placeholderProvider.tryCreateContent` is used to get access to the placeholders.
- If the properties Top and Bottom exist, they render inside the placeholders.
- The only difference between the top and bottom placeholders' code is of style definitions, and different variables are used in these placeholder's code.

In the above code, the "_onDispose()" method is used to dispose of or free up the memory.

```
private _onDispose(): void {

    console.log('[HelloWorldApplicationCustomizer._onDispose] Disposed
custom top and bottom placeholders.');

    }
```

11. Create a new file named `AppCustomizer.module.scss` (to define styling) under the `src\extensions\helloWorld` folder and add the code inside that file, as shown in the following screenshot:

```
TS HelloWorldApplicationCustomizer.ts        AppCustomizer.module.scss ×

src > extensions > helloWorld >  AppCustomizer.module.scss > .app > .bottom
  1    @import '~@microsoft/sp-office-ui-fabric-core/dist/sass/SPFabricCore.scss';
  2
  3    .app {
  4        .top {
  5            height:60px;
  6            text-align:center;
  7            line-height:2.5;
  8            font-weight:bold;
  9            display: flex;
 10            align-items: center;
 11            justify-content: center;
 12            background-color: $ms-color-themePrimary;
 13            color: $ms-color-white;
 14
 15        }
 16
 17        .bottom {
 18            height:40px;
 19            text-align:center;
 20            line-height:2.5;
 21            font-weight:bold;
 22            display: flex;
 23            align-items: center;
 24            justify-content: center;
 25            background-color: $ms-color-themePrimary;
 26            color: $ms-color-white;
 27        }
 28    }
```

Figure 10.5

12. Import styles in extension file `HelloWorldApplicationCustomizer.ts,` using the below command:
    `import styles from './AppCustomizer.module.scss';`

13. To test the application customizer, open `serve.json` located under config folder and update the properties section to include `Top` and `Bottom` messages, as shown in below screenshot:

```
TS HelloWorldApplicationCustomizer.ts    {} serve.json ×

config > {} serve.json > {} serveConfigurations
  1   {
  2       "$schema": "https://developer.microsoft.com/json-schemas/core-build/serve.schema.json",
  3       "port": 4321,
  4       "https": true,
  5       "serveConfigurations": {
  6           "default": {
  7               "pageUrl": "https://vipsitworld.sharepoint.com/sites/ModernTeamSite/SiteAssets/spfxextension.aspx",
  8               "customActions": {
  9                   "4a18dbc7-9fbd-4224-8ac7-f73aae162a97": {
 10                       "location": "ClientSideExtension.ApplicationCustomizer",
 11                       "properties": {
 12                           "Top": "Page Header",
 13                           "Bottom": "Page Footer"
 14                       }
 15                   }
 16               }
 17           },
 18           "helloWorld": {
 19               "pageUrl": "https://vipsitworld.sharepoint.com/sites/ModernTeamSite/SiteAssets/spfxextension.aspx",
 20               "customActions": {
 21                   "4a18dbc7-9fbd-4224-8ac7-f73aae162a97": {
 22                       "location": "ClientSideExtension.ApplicationCustomizer",
 23                       "properties": {
 24                           "Top": "Page Header",
 25                           "Bottom": "Page Footer"
 26                       }
 27                   }
 28               }
 29           }
 30       }
 31   }
```

Figure 10.6

14. In the command prompt, run the command – `gulp serve`

15. SharePoint site will open. Click on **Load debug scripts** (to load scripts from localhost), as shown in below screenshot:

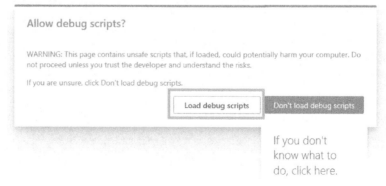

Figure 10.7

16. The following screenshot shows header and footer added on the page:

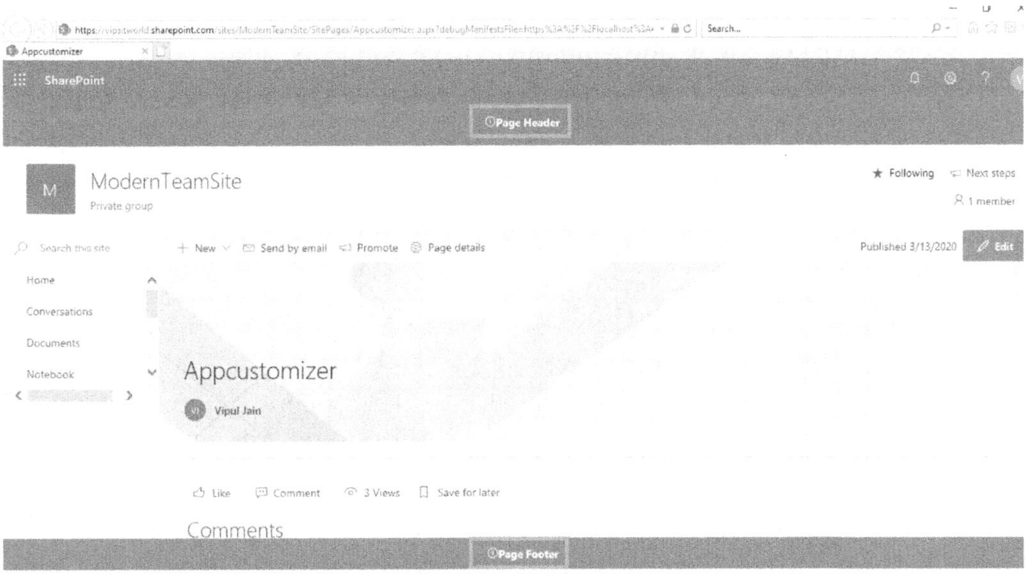

Figure 10.8

Always test SharePoint Framework extensions with new SharePoint pages.

Develop your first field customizer

Follow the below steps to develop your first field customizer:

1. Create a directory for SPFx solution using the below command:

   ```
   md spfx-fieldcustomizer
   ```

2. Navigate to the directory created in *Step 1* using the below command;

   ```
   cd spfx-fieldcustomizer
   ```

3. Use the below command to run Yeoman SharePoint Generator to create the solution:

   ```
   yo @microsoft/sharepoint
   ```

4. Provide below values in the Yeoman generator wizard:
   - **Solution Name:** Select default value by pressing *Enter*
   - **The target for the component:** SharePoint Online only (latest)
   - **Place of files:** Current folder
   - **Deployment option:** *N* to install on each site explicitly

- **Permission to access Web APIs:** N to avoid granting permissions to access Web APIs
- **Type of client-side component to create:** Extension
- **Type of client-side extension to create:** Field Customizer
- **Field Customizer name:** HelloWorld
- **Field Customizer description:** Select default value by pressing enter
- **The framework to choose:** No JavaScript Framework

5. Once the Yeoman generator finishes generating the solution, open the solution in Visual Studio Code editor using `code .` command.

6. Open `HelloWorldFieldCustomizer.manifest.json` in the `src\extensions\helloWorld` folder. This file contains information about `componentType`, `extensionType`, `alias`, and `id`, as shown in the following screenshot:

```
{} HelloWorldFieldCustomizer.manifest.json ×

src > extensions > helloWorld > {} HelloWorldFieldCustomizer.manifest.json > ...
  1  {
  2    "$schema": "https://developer.microsoft.com/json-schemas/spfx/client-side-extension-manifest.schema.json"
  3
  4    "id": "e6f987f4-a743-4ba8-b79d-f280deece1a8",
  5    "alias": "HelloWorldFieldCustomizer",
  6    "componentType": "Extension",
  7    "extensionType": "FieldCustomizer",
  8
  9    // The "*" signifies that the version should be taken from the package.json
 10    "version": "*",
 11    "manifestVersion": 2,
 12
 13    // If true, the component can only be installed on sites where Custom Script is allowed.
 14    // Components that allow authors to embed arbitrary script code should set this to true.
 15    // https://support.office.com/en-us/article/Turn-scripting-capabilities-on-or-off-1f2c515f-5d7e-448a-9fd7
 16    "requiresCustomScript": false
 17  }
 18
```

Figure 10.9

7. Open file `HelloWorldFieldCustomizer.ts`. By default, this file contains three methods:

- `onInit()`: This event occurs before the page DOM is ready. This method returns a promise that you can use to perform asynchronous operations. `onRenderCell()` is not called until the promise has been resolved.
- `onRenderCell()`: This event occurs when each cell is rendered. It provides event.domElement to customize the representation of the field.

- **onDisposeCell()**: This method can be used to free up any used resources (or memory) that were allocated during the rendering of the field to avoid any resource leak.

8. To test field customizer extension, you will need first to create the field/ column to test the customizer. Navigate to the site in your SharePoint Online tenant where you want to test the field customizer.

9. On the toolbar, select **New**, and then select **List**, as shown in the below screenshot:

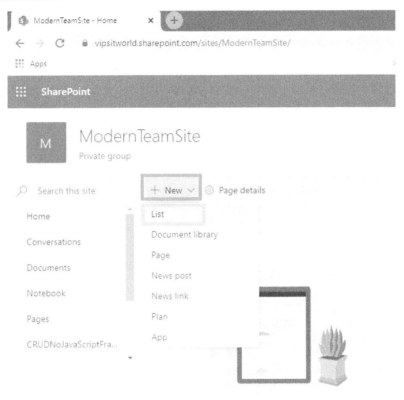

Figure 10.10

10. Create a new list named Employee, and then click on **Create**.

11. Select the plus sign, and then select **Number** to create a new number field for the list, as shown in the following screenshot:

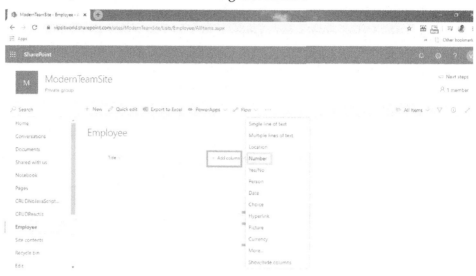

Figure 10.11

12. Give the name of the field as `PercentComplete`, and then click on **Save**, as shown in the following screenshot:

Figure 10.12

13. Add some list items in the SharePoint list.

14. Open `serve.json` file from the `config` folder. Update the `InternalFieldName` attribute as `PercentComplete` based on the field name, which we created in the previous step. Also, update the `pageUrl` attribute to match a URL of the list created in the previous steps.

The following screenshot shows the `serve.json` file:

```
{} serve.json  ×

config > {} serve.json > {} serveConfigurations > {} helloWorld > {} fieldCustomizers
  1  {
  2    "$schema": "https://developer.microsoft.com/json-schemas/core-build/serve.schema.json",
  3    "port": 4321,
  4    "https": true,
  5    "serveConfigurations": {
  6      "default": {
  7        "pageUrl": "https://vipsitworld.sharepoint.com/sites/ModernTeamSite/Lists/Employee/AllItems.aspx",
  8        "fieldCustomizers": {
  9          "PercentComplete": {
 10            "id": "e6f987f4-a743-4ba8-b79d-f280deece1a8",
 11            "properties": {
 12              "sampleText": "Value"
 13            }
 14          }
 15        }
 16      },
 17      "helloWorld": {
 18        "pageUrl": "https://vipsitworld.sharepoint.com/sites/ModernTeamSite/Lists/Employee/AllItems.aspx",
 19        "fieldCustomizers": {
 20          "PercentComplete": {
 21            "id": "e6f987f4-a743-4ba8-b79d-f280deece1a8",
 22            "properties": {
 23              "sampleText": "Value"
 24            }
 25          }
 26        }
 27      }
 28    }
 29  }
 30
```

Figure 10.13

15. In the command prompt, type the command – `gulp serve`.

16. Accept loading of debugging manifests by clicking **Load debug scripts**, as shown in the following screenshot:

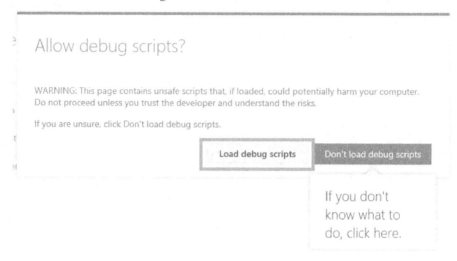

Figure 10.14

17. The following screenshot shows the formatted list column with an additional prefix string as **Value**:

Figure 10.15

18. Open the `HelloWorldFieldCustomizer.module.scss` file in the `src\extensions\helloWorld` folder, and update the styling definition as shown in the following screenshot:

```
{} serve.json    HelloWorldFieldCustomizer.module.scss ×
src > extensions > helloWorld > HelloWorldFieldCustomizer.module.scss > ...
.HelloWorld {
  .cell {
    background-color: "[theme:themePrimary, default:#e5e5e5]";
    display: 'inline-block';
  }
  .full {
    background-color: #e7e7e7;
    width: 100px;
  }
}
```

Figure 10.16

19. Open the `HelloWorldFieldCustomizer.ts` file in the `src\extensions\helloWorld` folder, and update the onRenderCell method, as shown in below screenshot:

```
@override
public onRenderCell(event: IFieldCustomizerCellEventParameters): void {
  // Use this method to perform your custom cell rendering.
  //const text: string = `${this.properties.sampleText}: ${event.fieldValue}`;
  //event.domElement.innerText = text;
  //event.domElement.classList.add(styles.cell);

  event.domElement.classList.add(styles.cell);
  event.domElement.innerHTML = `
          <div class='${styles.HelloWorld}'>
              <div class='${styles.full}'>
              <div style='width: ${event.fieldValue}px; background:#0094ff; color:#c0c0c0'>
                    ${event.fieldValue}
              </div>
              </div>
          </div>`;
}
```

Figure 10.17

20. Make sure gulp serve is running. Refresh the list view, and you will see the field will be displayed as progress completion, as shown in the following screenshot:

Figure 10.18

Develop a ListView Command Set extension

Follow the below steps to develop your first ListView Command Set extension:

1. Create a directory for SPFx solution using the below command:

   ```
   md spfx-listviewcommandset
   ```

2. Navigate to the directory created in Step 1 using the below command:

   ```
   cd spfx-listviewcommandset
   ```

3. Use the below command to run Yeoman SharePoint Generator to create the solution:

   ```
   yo @microsoft/sharepoint
   ```

4. Provide below values in the Yeoman generator wizard:
   - **Solution Name:** Select default value by pressing *Enter*
   - **The target for the component:** SharePoint Online only (latest)
   - **Place of files:** Current folder

- **Deployment option:** *N* to install on each site explicitly

- **Permission to access Web APIs:** *N* to avoid granting permissions to access Web APIs

- **Type of client-side component to create:** Extension

- **Type of client-side extension to create:** ListView Command Set

- **ListView Command Set name:** HelloWorld

- **ListView Command Set description:** Select default value by pressing *Enter*

5. Once the Yeoman generator finishes generating the solution, open the solution in Visual Studio Code editor using `code .` command.

6. Open `HelloWorldCommandSet.manifest.json` in the `src\extensions\ helloWorld` folder. This file contains information about `componentType`, `extensionType`, `alias`, and id, as shown in the following screenshot:

```
{} HelloWorldCommandSet.manifest.json ×

src > extensions > helloWorld > {} HelloWorldCommandSet.manifest.json
  1    {
  2      "$schema": "https://developer.microsoft.com/json-schemas/spfx/command-set-extension-manifest.schema.json"
  3
  4      "id": "2eaf53c3-226c-4a34-a404-6545653fd87d",
  5      "alias": "HelloWorldCommandSet",
  6      "componentType": "Extension",
  7      "extensionType": "ListViewCommandSet",
  8
  9      // The "*" signifies that the version should be taken from the package.json
 10      "version": "*",
 11      "manifestVersion": 2,
 12
 13      // If true, the component can only be installed on sites where Custom Script is allowed.
 14      // Components that allow authors to embed arbitrary script code should set this to true.
 15      // https://support.office.com/en-us/article/Turn-scripting-capabilities-on-or-off-1f2c515f-5d7e-448a-9fd7
 16      "requiresCustomScript": false,
 17
 18      "items": {
 19        "COMMAND_1": {
 20          "title": { "default": "Command One" },
 21          "iconImageUrl": "icons/request.png",
 22          "type": "command"
 23        },
 24        "COMMAND_2": {
 25          "title": { "default": "Command Two" },
 26          "iconImageUrl": "icons/cancel.png",
 27          "type": "command"
 28        }
 29      }
 30    }
 31
```

Figure 10.19

As shown in *Figure 10.19*, in the default template/solution, you get two different buttons: Command One and Command Two.

7. Open the `HelloWorldCommandSet.ts` file in the `src\extensions\helloWorld` folder. By default, this file contains three methods:

   - `onInit()`: This event occurs before the page DOM is ready. This method returns a promise that you can use to perform asynchronous operations. `onListViewUpdated()` is not called until the promise has been resolved.

   - `onListViewUpdated()`: This event occurs separately for each command. The `tryGetCommand` helps to get the command object, which is a representation of the command in UI.

     The following screenshot shows default `onListViewUpdated()` method:

```
@override
public onListViewUpdated(event: IListViewCommandSetListViewUpdatedParameters): void {
  const compareOneCommand: Command = this.tryGetCommand('COMMAND_1');
  if (compareOneCommand) {
    // This command should be hidden unless exactly one row is selected.
    compareOneCommand.visible = event.selectedRows.length === 1;
  }
}
```

Figure 10.20

   - `onExecute()`: This method defines what happens when a command is executed.

8. Open SharePoint site, create a new SharePoint list (you can use any existing list also) and add some test data, as shown in the following screenshot:

UserDirectory

Title ∨

Vipul Jain

BPB Publications

Figure 10.21

9. Open `serve.json` file located under the `config` folder. Update `PageUrl` to the list URL created in the previous step:

```
{} serve.json ×

config > {} serve.json > {} serveConfigurations > {} helloWorld > ▦ pageUrl
 1
 2    "$schema": "https://developer.microsoft.com/json-schemas/core-build/serve.schema.json",
 3    "port": 4321,
 4    "https": true,
 5    "serveConfigurations": {
 6      "default": {
 7        "pageUrl": "https://vipsitworld.sharepoint.com/sites/ModernTeamSite/Lists/UserDirectory/AllItems.aspx",
 8        "customActions": {
 9          "2eaf53c3-226c-4a34-a404-6545653fd87d": {
10            "location": "ClientSideExtension.ListViewCommandSet.CommandBar",
11            "properties": {
12              "sampleTextOne": "One item is selected in the list",
13              "sampleTextTwo": "This command is always visible."
14            }
15          }
16        }
17      },
18      "helloWorld": {
19        "pageUrl": "https://vipsitworld.sharepoint.com/sites/ModernTeamSite/Lists/UserDirectory/AllItems.aspx",
20        "customActions": {
21          "2eaf53c3-226c-4a34-a404-6545653fd87d": {
22            "location": "ClientSideExtension.ListViewCommandSet.CommandBar",
23            "properties": {
24              "sampleTextOne": "One item is selected in the list",
25              "sampleTextTwo": "This command is always visible."
26            }
27          }
28        }
29      }
30    }
```

Figure 10.22

As shown in Figure 10.22, you can set many properties inside `customActions`. The `location` property defines where the commands should be displayed. The possible values are `ClientSideExtension.ListViewCommandSet.ContextMenu`, `ClientSideExtension.ListViewCommandSet.CommandBar` and `ClientSideExtension. ListViewCommandSet`.

10. In the command prompt, type the command – `gulp serve`.

11. Accept loading of debugging manifests by clicking **Load debug scripts**, as shown in the following screenshot:

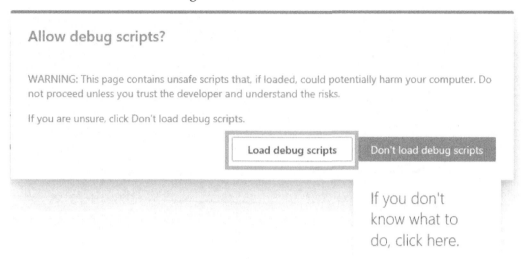

Figure 10.23

12. The **Command Two**-button will appear in the toolbar, as shown in the following screenshot:

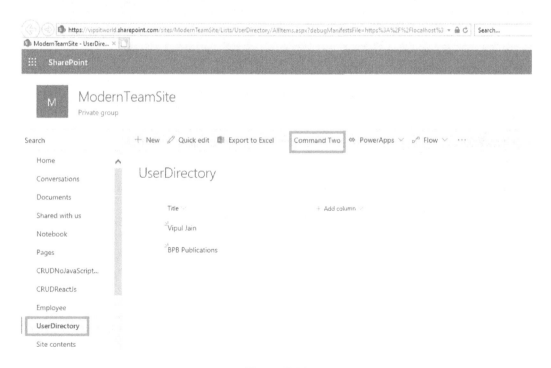

Figure 10.24

13. The **Command One**-button will not appear until you will select any list item, as shown in the following screenshot:

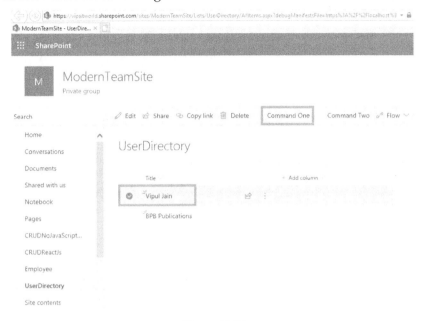

Figure 10.25

14. Click on **Command One**-button; it will display an alert, as shown in the following screenshot:

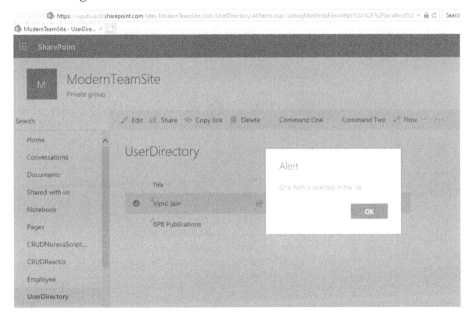

Figure 10.26

15. Open `HelloWorldCommandSet.ts` from the `src\extensions\helloWorld` folder and update `onExecute` method, as shown in the following screenshot:

```
@override
public onExecute(event: IListViewCommandSetExecuteEventParameters): void {
  switch (event.itemId) {
    case 'COMMAND_1':
      Dialog.alert(`${this.properties.sampleTextOne}`);
      break;
    case 'COMMAND_2':
      Dialog.prompt(`Clicked ${strings.Command2}. Enter something to alert:`).then((value: string) => {
        Dialog.alert(value);
      });
      break;
    default:
      throw new Error('Unknown command');
  }
}
```

Figure 10.27

16. Make sure that the gulp serve is running. Refresh the SharePoint list – UserDirectory and click on the **Command Two**-button. The following screenshot shows the output once the button is clicked:

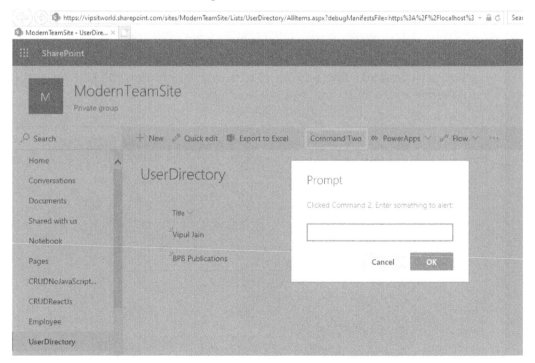

Figure 10.28

The preceding screenshot shows how buttons can be customized (for alerts and prompts) using the ListView Command Set SharePoint Framework extension.

Conclusion

In this chapter, we discussed SharePoint Framework extensions and its three types, that is, Application customizer, Field customizer, and ListView Command Set. These extensions help to expand SharePoint modern UI. The application customizer helps to extend the predefined placeholders (header/footer) on a SharePoint page. The field customizer helps to modify the representation of a field/column in a SharePoint list. ListView Command Set helps to extend the toolbar and context menu of a SharePoint list. In the next chapter, we will see how we can use Library components in SharePoint Framework.

Points to remember

- SharePoint Framework extensions can be tested on new SharePoint pages only.
- Field customizer by default provides three methods, that is, `onInit()`, `onRenderCell()` and `onDisposeCell()`.

Multiple Choice Questions

1. In which file the properties for field customizer are configured?

    a. config.json

    b. serve.json

    c. launch.json

    d. manifest.json

Answer

1. B

Questions

1. What are the different methods that the ListView Command Set extension class provides?

2. List the steps to change the header and footer of a modern new SharePoint page.

Key terms

- **SharePoint Framework extensions:** These are client-side components that allow extending the SharePoint user experience.

CHAPTER 11

Library Component Type in SharePoint Framework

Library Component Type was first introduced in SharePoint Framework version 1.8 with preview capabilities (beta features), and in SharePoint Framework version 1.9.1, Library Components were generally available. SharePoint Framework Library Component Type provides you an option to create shared code, which can be independently versioned and deployed in the SharePoint tenant.

In this chapter, we will see what Library Component Types are and how we can develop the Library Component Type in SharePoint Framework.

Structure

In this chapter, we will cover the following topics:
- Overview of Library Component Type
- Developing Library Component Type in SharePoint Framework

Objective

After studying this chapter, you should be able to:
- Understand the meaning of Library Component Type
- Develop your Library Component Type

Overview of Library Component Type

Using Library Component Type, you can create shared code and deploy it in SharePoint tenant. This shared code can be referenced across all SPFx components (Web Parts, Extensions, and so on) in the SharePoint tenant. You can create a Library Component solution by selecting Component Type as `Library` in the Yeoman scaffolding process. Library Components are not supported when the solution is deployed using the site collection app catalog.

The Library Component can be referenced in a SharePoint Framework solution by defining the dependency in the package.json file of the web part.

You can host only one Library Component version at a time in a tenant.

Developing Library Component Type in SharePoint Framework

Follow the below steps for creating a Library Component Type solution:

1. Create a directory for SPFx solution using the below command:

   `md spfx-librarycomponent-type`

2. Navigate to the directory created in Step 1 using the below command:

   `cd spfx-librarycomponent-type`

3. Use the below command to run Yeoman SharePoint Generator to create the solution:

   `yo @microsoft/sharepoint`

4. Provide the following values in the Yeoman generator wizard:

   - **Solution Name:** Select default value by pressing *Enter*
   - **The target for the component:** SharePoint Online only (latest)
   - **Place of files:** Current folder
   - **Deployment option:** *Y* to install on all sites
   - **Permission to access Web APIs:** *N* to avoid granting permissions to access Web APIs
   - **Type of client-side component to create:** Library
   - **Library name:** `customLibrary`
   - **Library description:** Select default value by pressing *Enter*

The following screenshot shows the options selected for the solution:

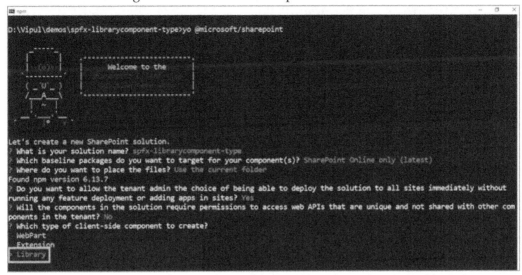

Figure 11.1

5. Once the Yeoman generator finishes generating the solution, open the solution in Visual Studio Code editor using `code .` command.

6. The solution will have an `index.ts` file that contains an export from the `CustomLibraryLibrary` created, as shown in the following screenshot:

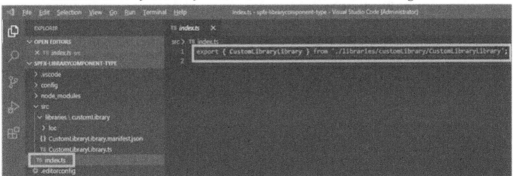

Figure 11.2

7. Open the file `CustomLibraryLibrary.ts` located under the `libraries\`
   `customLibrary` folder. You will find that a default method, name(), has been
   created. Rename this method, as shown in the below image:

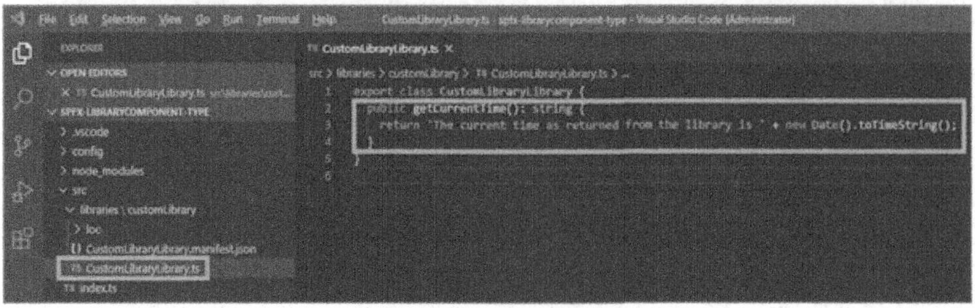

Figure 11.3

8. In the command prompt, run the command – `gulp serve` to verify the
   build process. If the build process is successful, this means that now you are
   ready to use the Libray to your SPFx web parts.

9. Run the below command to consume the Library Component Type (created
   in above steps), or to test the library component type locally:

   `npm link`

   Below is the screenshot of running the above command:

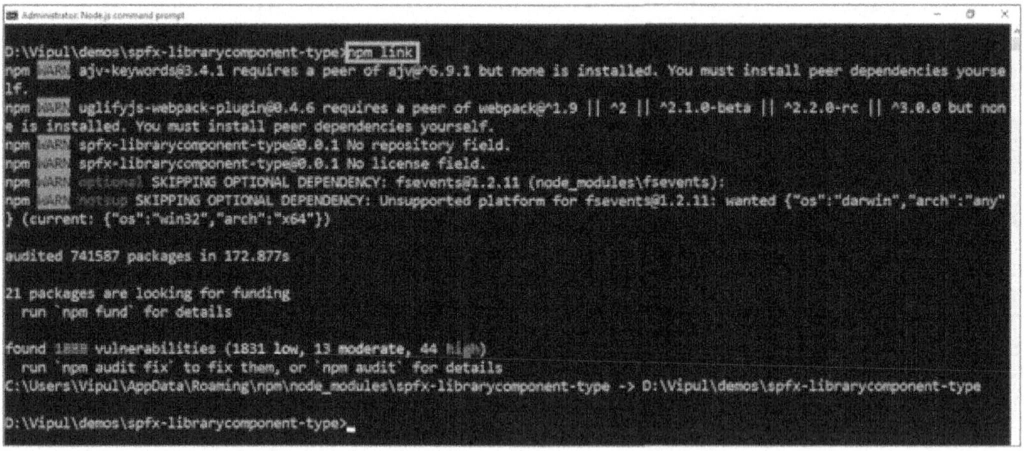

Figure 11.4

It will create a local npm link to the library with the name which is provided
in the `package.json`.

10. Create a web part project in a separate project folder (not in the library project
    folder structure).

11. From the root of the new web part folder, run the below command:

```
npm link spfx-librarycomponent-type
```

It will create a symbolic link to that locally built library into the web part and will make it available to your web part, as shown in the following screenshot:

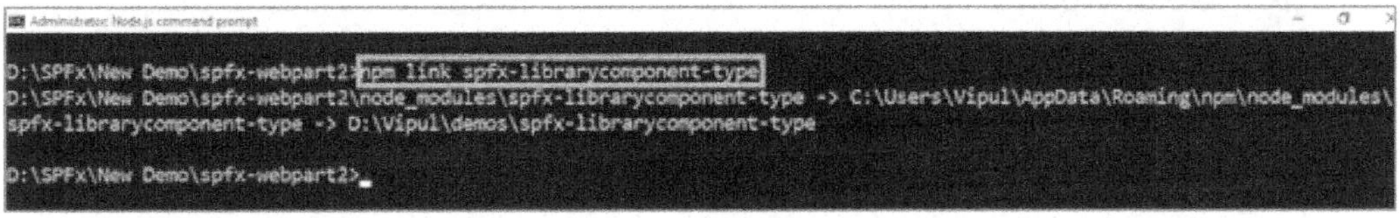

Figure 11.5

12. Open the web part solution in Visual Studio Code editor using `code .` command.

13. Add an import statement to refer to your custom library, as shown in the following screenshot:

Figure 11.6

14. Change the default `render()` method and call the custom library method `getCurrentTime()` by creating an instance. Call the method `myInstance.getCurrentTime()`, as shown in the following screenshot:

```
TS SpfxWebpart2WebPart.ts X

src > webparts > spfxWebpart2 > TS SpfxWebpart2WebPart.ts > 🎰 SpfxWebpart2WebPart > 𝒷 render
 9    import styles from './SpfxWebpart2WebPart.module.scss';
10    import * as strings from 'SpfxWebpart2WebPartStrings';
11
12    import * as myLibrary from 'spfx-librarycomponent-type';
13
14    export interface ISpfxWebpart2WebPartProps {
15      description: string;
16    }
17
18    export default class SpfxWebpart2WebPart extends BaseClientSideWebPart<ISpfxWebpart2WebPartProps> {
19
20      public render(): void {
21
22        const myInstance = new myLibrary.CustomLibraryLibrary();
23
24        this.domElement.innerHTML = `
25          <div class="${ styles.spfxWebpart2 }">
26            <div class="${ styles.container }">
27              <div class="${ styles.row }">
28                <div class="${ styles.column }">
29                  <span class="${ styles.title }">Welcome to SharePoint!</span>
30                  <p class="${ styles.subTitle }">Customize SharePoint experiences using Web Parts.</p>
31                  <p class="${ styles.description }">${escape(this.properties.description)}</p>
32                  <p>${myInstance.getCurrentTime()}</p>
33                  <a href="https://aka.ms/spfx" class="${ styles.button }">
34                    <span class="${ styles.label }">Learn more</span>
35                  </a>
36                </div>
37              </div>
38            </div>
39          </div>`;
40      }
```

Figure 11.7

15. To test your web part, run the command – `gulp serve`.

16. The web part will show current time (in local workbench) which is getting displayed from library component type, as shown in the following screenshot:

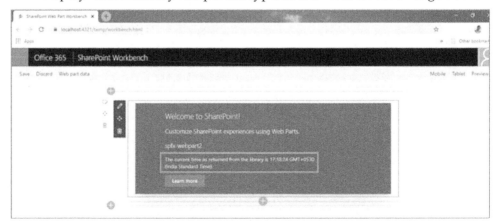

Figure 11.8

17. You can also deploy Library Component Type to your tenant App Catalog. Navigate to the library root folder and bundle and package the solution using below commands:

```
gulp bundle -ship
```

```
gulp package-solution -ship
```

It will build the solution and will create a `.sppkg` file, which is located in the `sharepoint\solution` folder.

18. Deploy this package in the tenant App Catalog and make it tenant wide deployed by checking the **Make this solution available to all sites in the organization** option, as shown in the following screenshot:

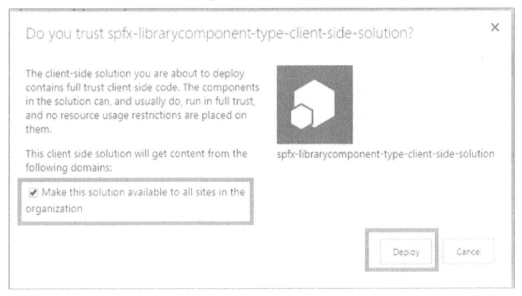

Figure 11.9

19. Navigate to the web part solution folder, and open the `package.json` file in the root of that folder.

20. Add an entry to reflect the library entry and its version to the dependencies section, as shown in the following screenshot:

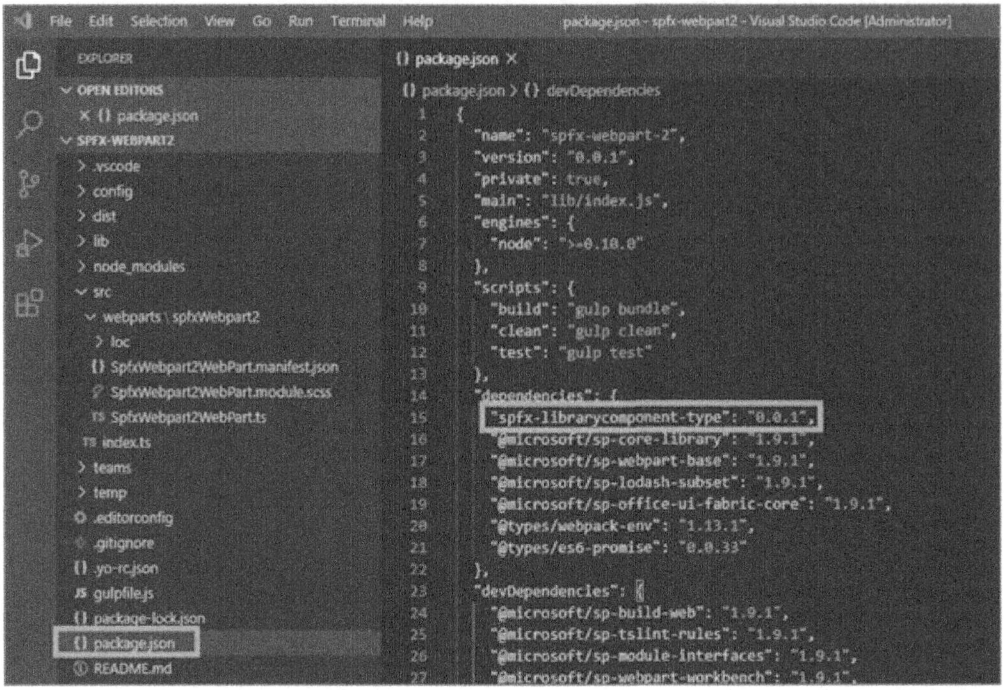

Figure 11.10

21. Build and package the web part using the following commands:

```
gulp bundle –ship
```

```
gulp package-solution –ship
```

22. Deploy the web part solution to the tenant App Catalog, as shown in the below screenshot:

Figure 11.11

23. Add the web part on a SharePoint page and observe that the web part is showing the same output when it is served locally.

The following screenshot shows the web part on a SharePoint page:

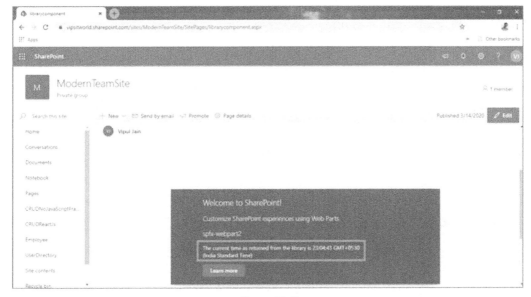

Figure 11.12

Below are the two important points: -

1. **If you make any changes to the library and publish the library to the app catalog again, the web part will be automatically updated without the need to rebuild/republish the web part.**

2. **If you want to unlink an SPFx library that is linked during development in your SPFx project, navigate to SPFx project root folder and run the below command:**

```
npm unlink <library-name>
```

Conclusion

In this chapter, we discussed Library Component Type and how you can use library code in SPFx web parts. We also discussed how you could link and unlink your library component with the SPFx web part. In the next chapter, we will discuss a few of the frequently asked questions in the SharePoint Framework.

Points to remember

- SharePoint Framework version 1.9.1 introduced the Library Component Type as a generally available feature to use in a production environment.
- You can only host one library component version at the time in a tenant.

Multiple Choice Questions

1. Which command helps to link a library to the web part project?

    a. gulp serve

    b. gulp bundle --ship

    c. gulp package-solution --ship

    d. npm link

Answer

1. D

Questions

1. How can you unlink a library component type with an SPFx web part?

2. List down steps to link a library to and an SPFx web part project.

Key terms

- **Library Component Type:** Library Component Type provides you an option to create shared code, which can be independently versioned and deployed in the SharePoint tenant.

CHAPTER 12
Frequently Asked Questions in SharePoint Framework

1. Which version is supported in SharePoint 2019?

Answer: SharePoint 2019 only supports the version that matches the server-side dependencies of the deployed packages. You can use SharePoint Framework v1.4.1 while working with SharePoint 2019.

2. Which version is supported in SharePoint 2016?

Answer: When you are targeting the SharePoint 2016 platform, you need to use the SharePoint Framework v1.1.0 due to the server-side version dependencies.

3. How can I lock down the exact versions of different dependencies in my solution?

Answer: You can do this using the command - `npm shrinkwrap`. You can find the information about the exact versions used in the `npm-shrinkwrap.json` file, which gets available in the solution's root folder.

4. How can I check what version of the SharePoint Framework I am using?

Answer: In the command prompt, type the command - `npm ls -g --depth=0`. Check the version of the @microsoft/generator-sharepoint package.

If you don't see it, then you don't have the SharePoint Framework Yeoman generator installed in your machine.

Following is the screenshot showing the output of running the above command in my machine:

```
Administrator: Node.js command prompt

D:\>npm ls -g --depth=0
C:\Users\Vipul\AppData\Roaming\npm
+-- @microsoft/generator-sharepoint@1.10.0
+-- corporate-library@0.0.1 -> D:\SPFx\Library Component Type\corporate-library
+-- gulp@4.0.2
+-- library-component@0.0.1 -> D:\SPFx\New Demo\library-component
+-- npm@6.13.7
+-- spfx-librarycomponent-type@0.0.1 -> D:\Vipul\demos\spfx-librarycomponent-type
+-- webpack@4.41.5
`-- yo@3.1.1
```

Figure 12.1

5. How do I implement elevated permissions in SPFx web parts?

Answer: Business use cases (functionalities) that require elevated permissions should be developed in provider-hosted add-ins and then exposed as REST services, which then can be called from SPFx web parts.

6. Which languages should I learn to start developing SPFx web parts?

Answer: You should learn TypeScript for building SPFx web parts. Also, learn React JS, which is best suited for SPFx web parts as there are various controls like Office Fabric UI (Fluent UI) React components for developers to start using.

7. Can I use SharePoint Framework on classic SharePoint sites?

Answer: You can use SharePoint Framework client-side web parts on classic SharePoint, meaning classic team sites and publishing sites. However, you cannot use SharePoint Framework extensions as they are only available in the new SharePoint sites.

8. How can I enable the site collection level App Catalog?

Answer: Follow the below steps to enable site collection level App Catalog:

    a) Download and install SharePoint Online Management Shell.

    b) Connect to your SharePoint Admin Portal using the following command:
    Connect-SPOService

    c) Enter the URL for your SharePoint Admin Portal.

d) Enter the credentials of the user who has permission to manage SharePoint from SharePoint Admin Center.

e) Press *Enter*.

f) Type the following command in SharePoint Online Management Shell to get the instance of the site collection:

```
$site = Get-SPOSite <Site Collection Url>
```

g) Press *Enter*.

h) Then type the below command to configure the App Catalog in your site collection:

```
Add-SPOSiteCollectionAppCatalog -Site $site
```

i) Press *Enter*.

j) Once done with the steps above, you should see a library named **"Apps for SharePoint"** in your site collection site contents.

9. What is the difference between reactive and non-reactive property pane?

Answer: In reactive mode, on every change in property pane control, a change event gets triggered. Reactive behavior automatically updates the web part with the new values. The non-reactive mode does not update the web part automatically unless the user confirms the changes by clicking on the **Apply** button, which gets enabled in non-reactive mode only.

To enable non-reactive mode, add the below code in your web part:

```
protected get disableReactivePropertyChanges(): boolean {
return true;
    }
```

10. How can I validate web part property values?

Answer: Let's say you have a description property in your web part property pane and you want to check its value which should not be longer than 30 characters, then you can write below `private` method in main web part file (.ts file):

```
private validateDescription(value: string): string {
    if (value === null ||
      value.trim().length === 0) {
      return 'Provide a description';
    }
```

```
        if (value.length > 30) {

            return 'Description should not be longer than 40
characters';

        }


        return '';

    }
```

You can associate the above method with the description web part property in getPropertyPaneConfiguration method as shown in below code:

```
protected getPropertyPaneConfiguration():
IPropertyPaneConfiguration {
    return {
        pages: [
            {
                header: {
                    description: strings.PropertyPaneDescription
                },
                groups: [
                    {
                        groupName: strings.BasicGroupName,
                        groupFields: [
                            PropertyPaneTextField('description', {
                                label: strings.DescriptionFieldLabel,
                                onGetErrorMessage: this.
validateDescription.bind(this)
                            })
                        ]
                    }
                ]
            }
        ]
    };
}
```

11. How to set the default value for web part property pane?

Answer: In `manifest.json` file (that describes the web part), the `preconfigured Entries` property defines an array of properties, which includes title, description, and so on. In the same array, in properties, you can specify the default values for web part properties as key-value pair, as shown in the following screenshot:

```
"preconfiguredEntries": [{
  "groupId": "1edbd9a8-0bfb-4aa2-9afd-14b8c45dd489", // Discover
  "group": { "default": "Under Development" },
  "title": { "default": "Gallery" },
  "description": { "default": "Shows items from the selected list" },
  "officeFabricIconFontName": "Page",
  "properties": {
    "description": "Gallery"
  }
}]
```

Figure 12.2

12. How to add a second web part to an existing SharePoint Framework project?

Answer: To add a new Web Part to your existing SharePoint Framework project, call the SharePoint Yeoman generator on your existing SharePoint Framework project. The Yeoman generator will automatically detect that it's running on an existing project and will not scaffold the whole project. Instead, it will skip directly to add a new Web Part. Once you answer the standard web part questions like title, description, and so on, the SharePoint Framework Yeoman generator will add the new Web Part to the project and will register it with the project's configuration.

Consider the scenario – I created a web part "`helloWorld`" in an SPFx project with the name – `SECONDTRY` in which I added a web part, as shown in the below screenshot:

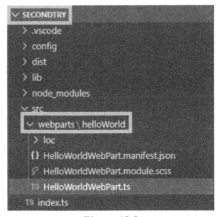

Figure 12.3

Now I want to add one more web part in the same project (that is, SECONDTRY). I will run the SharePoint Yeoman generator on my existing SPFx project, and a second web part will be added.

Following is the image showing that Yeoman generator skipped all other steps and just asked about web part related questions:

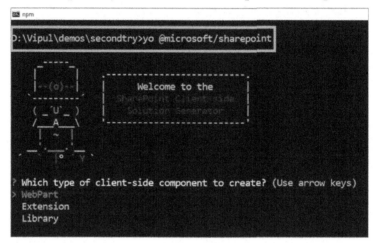

Figure 12.4

Following is the image showing that a second web part (secondHelloWorld) has been added in the same SPFx project:

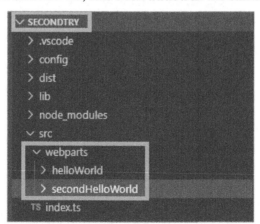

Figure 12.5

In the config/config.json file, check that there should be separate entries for the number of web parts added, especially in "bundles" and "localizedResources" properties.

13. How does SharePoint Framework know which Web Part to run if there are multiple web parts in a single SPFx project?

Answer: The combination of Web Part manifest file, Web Part code file (.ts file), an entry in the config.json file instructs SharePoint where to get the code for the particular Web Part and hence accordingly, particular web part renders based on data in these three files.

14. How can I get information about what is getting released with the SharePoint Framework?

Answer: The following table lists some of the hyperlinks to get updated on SharePoint development topics:

Title	Hyperlink
SharePoint Development Blog	**https://developer.microsoft.com/en-us/office/blogs/**
SharePoint Development Community	**https://docs.microsoft.com/en-us/sharepoint/dev/community/community**
SharePoint YouTube video channel	**https://www.youtube.com/channel/UC_mKdhw-V6CeCM7gTo_Iy7w**
SharePoint on Twitter	**https://twitter.com/sharepoint**

Table 12.1

Made in the USA
Monee, IL
23 June 2021